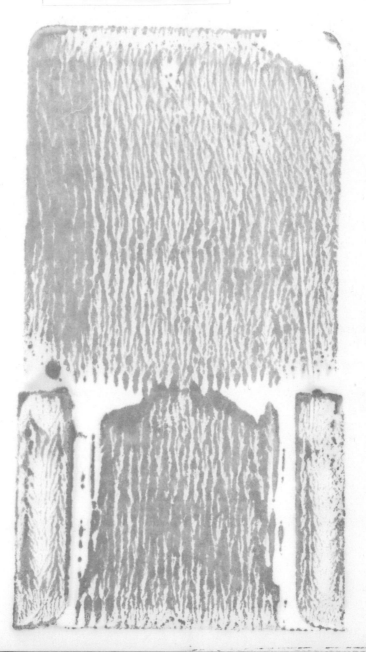

The Buried Treasure
of Archaeology

The Buried Treasure

# of Archaeology

by Louis A. Brennan

RANDOM HOUSE   NEW YORK

The drawings on pages 5, 109, 130, 131, 147, 181, 182, 202, 205, 211, and 228, made by Ingrid Fetz, originally appeared in *No Stone Unturned,* by Louis A. Brennan, © Copyright, 1959, by Random House, Inc.

Contents

The Buried Treasure of Archaeology

1

Archaeology Only Begins with Digging

B ECAUSE MANY B OOKS about archaeology have
given a somewhat misleading impression of what
it is, the best way to begin another about it is to make
clear what it is by describing what it does and does not
try to do.

Archaeology is not, though it often seems so, the mere
digging up of odds and ends of the past for their odd-
ness, such as the charm stones of the early American
Indians; nor for their antiquity, like the 400,000-year-old
stone hand-axes of Olduvai Gorge in Africa; nor for their
sheer value, like the gold and silver treasure of the sand-

buried ship at Sutton Hoo, in England.

Nor do archaeologists sweat it out under their sun helmets only to fill museum cases with strange bric-a-brac, with mummies and war shields, with bronze urns and the altars of animal-headed idols. To put it simply, archaeology is the decoding of the secret book of pre-history (and sometimes of lost history) as it is written in the language of things found, on the clay or loam or gravel pages of the earth.

Archaeology only begins with digging. Along with this spade work goes the accurate recording and often enough the painstaking restoration of the specimens dug. This done, only after long study can the archaeologist proceed to his real task—interpretation. He must translate his specimens, as though they were words, into the story of what happened here, on the site of his dig, and to what people it happened, and what then happened to those people. For the proper science and study of mankind, it has long been recognized, is man. Archaeology takes as its study man as he once was.

Suppose, for instance, that an archaeologist is digging into the gravels of an ancient river and he comes upon a series of hand-axes. These are sometimes heart-shaped, sometimes more pointed tools of chipped stone from three to eight or nine inches long, with at least one sharp or cutting edge and a butt at the top for holding in the hand. The hand-ax is probably the grandfather of all tools and included in its simple shape is the principle of every hand tool we now possess. But there is no modern tool like it to tell us exactly how it was used. We only know it was probably used for nearly every task that confronted its maker.

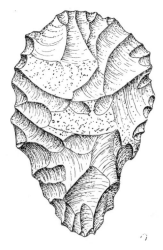

Hand-ax of about 200,000 years ago. Tools resembling this one have been found in America.

What were these tasks? The archaeologist looks over the data at his site on climate, environment and geology, and decides that the hand-ax would have been very useful to early man as a weapon for hand-to-hand conflict with a human enemy, or the giant pig of that day. It would have been useful as a cleaver to hack chunks of meat from the pig's carcass, to feed his family; and it could then have been used to crack the bones, to extract the nutritious marrow. It would have been useful as a sort of spade or hand hoe to grub for burrowing animals, or for edible roots. And, plainly enough, from its shape, it would have been useful as an ax-adze-knife to cut and shape wooden shafts. This seemed at one time to be enough explanation of the hand-ax, until a South African archaeologist came up with an even further use: as a sort of climber's pick, to be jabbed into tree trunks as early man scrambled up them after fruit or to escape danger.

Archaeologists have to do this kind of interpretation over and over. Sometimes it is with objects as seeming-simple as the hand-ax. Sometimes it is with objects well enough understood in themselves but not understood in their grouping or placement.

Such a problem was presented to American archaeologists when they first came upon Amerind (prehistoric American Indian) graves wherein the buried body was accompanied by broken objects—broken spear points, broken pots, or broken ornaments. Once they became aware, as grave after grave yielded broken objects, that the breakage was deliberate, they had to ask themselves why. The answer they arrived at was that these objects had been "killed" at the time of burial so as to release their spirits to enter the Happy Hunting Ground with their owner. He would need them.

Was this explanation a stroke of genius on the part of some very imaginative archaeologist? Not at all. These paltry spearheads in the graves of Amerind warriors, and the poor little pots in the graves of Amerind squaws, were exactly like what the great archaeologist Sir Leonard Woolley had found in the astounding tombs of Ur.

Chaplet of gold beech leaves and carnelian and lapis lazuli beads

Silver ring

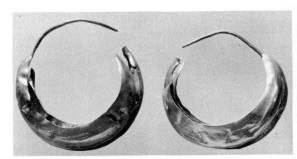

Gold earrings

Necklace of gold and lapis lazuli beads

All of these were found at Ur in the grave of a lady-in-waiting of Queen Shubad

The Metropolitan Museum of Art, Excavations of the University of Pennsylvania Museum and the British Museum, 1927-1928; Dodge Fund, 1933.

Here the deceased—obviously the rich and high-born—had as grave companions their own human servants who had been actually buried alive with them, in order to serve them in the next world. Lesser notables had the company of two or three deliberately killed underlings, perhaps slaves, perhaps relatives. But into the tomb of the King of Ur, alive and on their own legs, went some 60 to 70 members of the royal court, clothed in their finest and bearing musical instruments. Following them came the King's chariots and carts drawn by horses and asses from the royal stables and driven by royal charioteers and grooms. When all were assembled they drank a drugged potion, lay down with their dead lord, and smothered to death as tons of earth were shoveled in to cover the grave.

Killed servants and "killed" implements, these are the things an archaeologist must weave together by the thousands, to arrive at a portrayal of what human events took place here, the dirt of which he trowels and sifts through so carefully. The portrayal, not the things themselves, is the buried treasure of archaeology. A king was buried here, or a peaceful village was overwhelmed by wild tribesmen from the hills, or eight spearmen killed a mammoth and the members of their band feasted for weeks on its meat. Yes, such a thing did happen, 10,000 years ago, near Naco, Arizona. With nothing more than hand-thrown javelins, eight Amerind hunters brought down a Columbian mammoth at least ten feet high at the shoulder, and they did this not for sport but because it was their way of making a living.

But to interpret a site is not enough for the archaeologist-prehistorian. Where does the site, where do the people who lived and died there, fit into the course of prehistory, into the story of mankind?

Now the archaeologist-prehistorian has to begin theorizing. He gives answers, that are really more or less reasoned guesses, to larger and ever larger questions about the relations of his site people to the human race. And eventually archaeology tries to answer the very largest of all questions: Where did man himself come from? How long has he been man? How did he manage to populate all the areas of the earth from the locale of his origin, if it was a single locale? The prehistorian cannot be content until he knows all the answers, and this is impossible, because he can never have all the facts. But if he can never have all the facts then he must make do with theory.

Scientists can no more cease to think up theories than they can voluntarily give up breathing. Every hard-won answer in science is but another way of asking the next question; just as every question, properly asked, suggests an answer. Maybe not the right one, but an answer.

One of the very large questions of prehistory about which theories have had to be constructed is how and when North and South America came to be populated. It is almost certain there were no early men here at the

9

time Swanscombe Man lived in England some 250,000 years ago. Zinjanthropus—East Africa Man—has been dated to a million and three-quarters years ago. We can only conclude, therefore, that some of these more primitive men must have traveled on foot across Asia until they came to the land that is now nearest America—eastern Siberia. Then what? Fifty miles of stormy, cold water now lie between eastern Siberia and western Alaska, with two islands—the Diomedes—in between.

But about twelve thousand years ago, when the oceans of the world were 300 to 400 feet lower than they are now, eastern Asia and Alaska were not separated by the cold waves of Bering Strait. They were one big territory, four or five times as big as Texas. A band of hunters could have walked from Siberia to Canada and not come within 500 miles of salt water.

But what good would it have done them? For at that time the last great glacier, called the Wisconsin, covered all of Canada. The glacier itself was the reason that the level of the ocean was so low, for an enormous amount of water was locked up in the ice of this glacier. Odd as it seems, however, there was no lowland glacier in Alaska or in northern Siberia. If man could survive the cold he could live in Alaska or Siberia well enough. There was plenty of game to eat—great mammoths and huge bison, the musk ox, and many other animals.

So, we now have the theory that man came to America afoot during the period of the Wisconsin glacier, waited around in Alaska until the ice melted, drifted south to what is now the United States, and kept going, to the very tip of South America.

But have we taken into account all the facts? Unfortunately for our theory we have not. The glacier had not melted enough for a way through to be open 15,000 years ago, and possibly not until 13,000 or even 12,000 years ago. How, then, did men get to the very tip of South America 6,000 miles distant at about 11,000 years ago? We know he did, through modern dating methods. How is it that Amerinds were hunting mammoths in Arizona 12,000 years ago, and almost certainly 15,000 years ago?

Very well. Let the theory be changed. Man came to America during the beginning stages of the Wisconsin glacier, while he could still walk on dry land from Siberia to Alaska, but before the glacier had closed off the way south. While more and more archaeologists are beginning to think this way, many doubt it. (Such a theory would have man in America 40,000 to 60,000 years ago, depending on which scientist's word is accepted as to when the Wisconsin began.)

The evidence for any such ancient Amerinds, it is argued, is much too slim. Where are the camp sites and bones of these 40,000- to 60,000-year-old people? In Europe, bones and tools of the 30,000- to 125,000-year-old Neanderthal cave men of the Wisconsin period have been found from Germany to Iraq; they are almost plentiful.

It is true that evidence of a 40,000-year-old Amerind

is scarce, but it exists—it will be discussed in this book —and what is made of it is a matter of what theory strikes your fancy.

Some day the facts that will prove when man first came to America will be unearthed and there will need be no more theories about it. This will not bring theorizing to a stop, even on this question. For there is now no knowledge gained that does not in a sense, create more ignorance. That is, we learn how much more is not known through learning itself. Only those who know very little can "know it all."

The human mind is the originator of science. Yet science as we think of it now, the deliberate pursuit of new knowledge, is only a few hundred years old. Most of what is now considered the proper concern of science, such as the motions of the heavenly bodies and the formation of the earth, was once not so considered. Various religions had various explanations for all these matters, and that was that.

It was, usually, not in the spirit of trying to disprove anything that men of scientific bent, beginning with the Greeks, began to find flaws in the accepted views. It was only because they could not prevent themselves from observing, interpreting, theorizing, and then inquiring further to see how their theories stood up, that they arrived at new and sometimes startling ideas.

Archaeology is not different from its sister sciences in its development out of educated guess and unsuspected ignorance into a tested body of knowledge with ever

STONEHENGE

Built in the dawn of English civilization, this circle of monoliths is over 3,000 years old. It stands on the Salisbury Plain less than two hours from London.

improving methods of adding to that knowledge. How this happened is best seen in the growth of knowledge about the prehistory of the famous Stonehenge site, in England.

THE MYSTERY OF STONEHENGE

In southern England, at Wiltshire, north of Salisbury, there stands on a plain a great circle of about 150 huge rough-hewn stones, each weighing up to 28 tons and rising to heights of 30 feet. The stones themselves are enclosed in a circular ditch and embankment about 320 feet in diameter. Some of these stones are still in what was apparently their original position: a great stone rests flat across two upright stones, standing apart, so that a mighty doorway is formed. Taken altogether in its original state, this great circle of stone doorways could only have been a rude but magnificent unroofed temple.

For a long time Stonehenge was thought to have been magically erected by Merlin, King Arthur's wizard. The first man who sought seriously to give a natural explanation for it was John Aubrey. He examined it in 1689, correctly judged it to be a ceremonial and religious center, and immediately pronounced it Druidical in origin. What right of fact had he to pronounce it Druidical? None that we would recognize today. But according to what was then known, it was a very sound guess.

The Druids were a class of priest-judges among the Celts. They held sacred the evergreen mistletoe, which they cut with a golden sickle, and they offered human sacrifice by burning victims in wicker baskets. Though some "sacrifices" were undoubtedly executions for crimes, the Druids being judges, others were for the purpose of augury. That is, human beings were killed, as among many peoples animals have been killed, so that the future could be foretold by certain signs that were thought to be revealed only at death.

The first historical mention of Druids was about 200 B.C., but what is actually known about them is not much more than is reported here. It is scarcely any wonder that Aubrey related this ancient, mysterious priesthood to the ancient, mysterious temple of Stonehenge. At least it was the relation of one fact (historical) with another (observational). And this Druidical theory became the commonly accepted truth about Stonehenge. Indeed, a man of wide education named William Stukeley devoted the last 40 years of his long life to working it out in detail without any suspicion that it was wrong.

A scholar who had taken both a medical degree and Holy Orders, Stukeley began in 1720 to exercise both his scientific and his religious training on interpreting the great temple. Mostly out of his imagination he recreated the Druidical religion as a kind of predecessor to Christianity, for which there is no supporting evidence at all. Much more successful were his scientific labors.

A thorough and gifted worker, Stukeley measured every stone in the temple and the distances between, around, and beyond the stones. Out of these measurements he created a fantastic ancient world, called by some Druidiotic. But the measurements themselves have been invaluable to archaeologists ever since, and one discovery by Stukeley opened up, eventually, the whole mystery of Stonehenge.

Working as he did for 40 years, Stukeley observed that there was one stone, which he called the Hele (sun) stone, directly over which the sun rose on Midsummer's

Day (now June 22, and the longest day of the year). His measurements showed that the original temple had been laid out on a base line that was the course of the sun across the sky on Midsummer's Day. From this he deduced that the builders of Stonehenge were sun worshippers.

He still thought, of course, that these sun worshippers were Druids. Not until 1901 did it become certain that if the builders were sun worshippers, they were certainly not Druids. It had been noted that while the sun arose over the Hele Stone on Midsummer's Day it did not rise over it precisely. In 1901 Sir Norman Lockyer, British Royal Astronomer, sat down and calculated the date at which the Midsummer Day sun had last risen precisely over the Hele Stone. It was June 24, 1680 B.C.

So, advances in the science of astronomy had contributed something to the Stonehenge story. But exactly what? The whole relationship between the Hele Stone and Midsummer's Day might be coincidence. Archaeologists had to wait another 50 years for further information, until the development by atomic physicists of the Carbon 14 dating method.

Carbon 14 is a radioactive form of carbon present in the air and taken in during its lifetime by all living matter, from shellfish to tree leaves. The age of anything once living (and still in existence) can be ascertained, up to about 50,000 years, by laboratory preparation and then testing it by Geiger counter. (C14, being radioactive, continuously breaks down or decays, the flashes of this breaking down are counted, and mathematics gives the result in years old.)

In 1950 some charcoal from a hole known to date from Stonehenge's founding was given a C14 test. The answer came out to 1845 B.C., plus or minus 275 years. This means that the wood from which the charcoal had come had been a living tree between 1845 B.C. plus 275 years (or 2120 B.C.) and 1845 B.C. minus 275 years (or 1570 B.C.). There was, of course, no way of telling how old the tree was at the time its wood was burned. But one fact is clear. The Royal Astronomer's calculated date of 1680 B.C. falls fairly within the C14 dates.

No, Stonehenge was not built by the Druids. It was laid out, probably, by the Stone Age farmer-herdsmen at about 2,000 B.C. Nor did the Druids enlarge it to its stage of greatest splendor. That was done either by the Beaker Folk, who made the beaker-shaped pottery that gave them their name, or during the time of their passage through the land, as traders in beaker-ware and bronze. Even the last phase of its importance was not Druidical. A dagger styled like those carried by Mycenaean Greeks of the Bronze Age was found carved on one of the standing stones. These Greeks were sun worshippers, too.

After hundreds of years of use and many periods of repair, Stonehenge fell into disuse and neglect. By the time the Druids came to England it was a semi-ruin.

Now that its origin has been cleared up archaeologists will admit that the Druids may have used this venerable semi-ruin, but only as they found it, and with super-

17

stitious awe. For the founders of Stonehenge were as ancient to the Druids as the Druids are to us.

Despite all that has been discovered about Stonehenge in the last 270 or more years, it is still by no means completely interpreted. Stuart Piggott, the archaeologist who conducted the last excavation there that produced the charcoal for C14 dating, dug up only half the site. The other half he left for some later investigation, when a new scientific tool, another C14, or a new breakthrough in knowledge would yield more information about Stonehenge than he could get from it now.

Nothing could make plainer than this decision of Piggott's what the archaeologist is really after. It is not more things, but more knowledge, and he will not dig for things if there is a chance it will destroy knowledge.

The field for the archaeologist's labor is therefore vast. It is all of prehistory. The distinction between history and prehistory is sharp and clear. Whatever there is a written record of—that is history. The archaeologist has many duties to perform within historic time, where no records were kept or they were lost. But here he is only a helper. Of prehistory he is the sole producer. Until he digs it up and interprets it, using geologists and other scientists to help him, it does not exist. After he has dug it up, then it becomes, if not history, the roots from which history grows.

If the line between history and prehistory is sharp and clear, it is by no means a straight line in time. The

Western Hemisphere did not become a part of history until 1492, some 5,000 years after the writing of the first records in Sumer and Egypt, which we can read, and the records of the Great India cities of Mohenjo-Daro and Harappa, which we cannot read. And not until more than 300 years later did all of what is now the United States become history. In 1807 Lewis and Clark returned from their expedition across the continent and only then did the people of the new nation know there were such things as the Rocky Mountains.

So it was when Caesar invaded Britain. He was both historical and historian. But the Britons, except for those about whom Caesar wrote, remained completely pre-historical because they were completely illiterate.

It is at this ragged borderline between history and prehistory that the portrayals from archaeology in this book will begin. From there they will go back as far in time as there is trace of man.

2

Long Swords and Long Ships

WHEREVER WE CROSS THE BORDER between history and prehistory in Western Europe we are bound to come face to face with one of three great fighting races: the Celts, the Teutons or Germanic tribes, and the sea-going Norse, or Vikings.

Warriors of the long sword, who rode their spike-wheeled war chariots with their long manes and mustaches of red or blond hair streaming behind, the Celts seem to have the deepest roots in prehistory of the three. For a thousand years they rampaged over Europe, from Asia Minor to France, and finally to Ireland, westernmost

outpost of Europe, whose people are called Gaels to
this day.

Some three centuries before Christ they had sacked
Rome. Having no use for it as a city, they immediately
retired to their villages in the forests, just like American
Indians after a raid. They are not heard of again until
they appear as the Helvetians of Caesar's *Commentaries.*

At the time Caesar attacked them the Helvetians were
seriously considering a move to France, where their
Celtic relatives lived. They were being menaced from
the east by the tough Illyrians and from the north by the
fierce Germanic tribes. Their defeat by Caesar made up
the minds of the survivors and they fled westward, the
only way open to them. Some kept moving, and crossed
the English channel into Britain. Though this was the
second wave of Celts to swarm into the British Isles, it
seems likely that it was the one that brought the Druids
to perform their mysteries at Stonehenge.

It was the presence of these Celts across the narrow
channel from France, close enough to give aid to their
French kinsmen, that decided Caesar on Britain's con-
quest. The Roman influence he set up there lasted for
five centuries. All England within the Roman wall became Latinized and therefore historical. Beyond, in the
rugged country of Wales and Scotland and in Ireland,
the Celts went about their business as though writing
had not been invented. Likewise, held in check only by
garrisons of Roman legions, the Germanic tribes seethed
in the forests of Continental Europe, erupting frequently

but never quite able to overwhelm the center of the civilized world.

This human wall between the keepers of almost the whole culture of man up to that time and destructive ignorance was broken through in A.D. 476. In that year the last Roman Emperor was banished from his throne by the Germanic chieftain Odoacer, and the Dark Ages began for all of Europe. This period is as much the field of the archaeologist as is the Stone Age.

Now the Germanic tribes began to rampage as the Celts had done before them. Different parts of Britain fell to the Angles, who gave England (Angle-land) their name, to the Saxons, after whom a German duchy is named, and the Jutes, who crossed the North Sea from Jutland. (The name Britain, however, comes from the Celtic tribal name, the Brythoni.)

These conquerors were not to remain too long in comfortable possession of the petty kingdoms they had carved out. Three centuries at most. By A.D. 800 the Vikings, warriors of the long sword, riding their dragon-prowed ships, had begun to practice piracy as far west-over-sea (as they called it) as Ireland.

Some authorities say that Viking means Man of the Fjord, a fjord being a long, narrow bay jutting into the coastline between two mountain ridges. The coasts of both Vestfold (Norway) and Ostefold (Sweden), land of the Vikings, are one fjord after another. Still other authorities say Viking means, simply, warrior. Both meanings fit these Norsemen. During spring seed-time they planted the fields of their narrow farms in the fjord valleys to grain. Then, while the crops were making under the summer sun, they followed the sea path in their long ships, to wherever the winds and their helmsmen took them, for adventure and for booty. And which they relished more would be hard to say.

It is small wonder that the Vikings of A.D. 800 behaved like the Angles and Saxons of A.D. 300 or the Celts of 500 B.C. They were all very little different in descent or language. All had in them the blood of those tomahawk-swinging horsemen who charged into Western Europe about 2000 B.C. from the Russian steppes. These invaders are known to archaeology as the Battle-Ax people, and they brought with them a language that is the parent of the languages spoken all over Western Europe and in America today. All the Germanic-type languages (of which English is one) and the Romance languages (those allied to Latin, such as Italian and French) are held by scholars to belong to a single language group called the Indo-European or the Aryan.

Loud and emphatic in their speech these Battle-Axers must have been. No words we actually know of survive from the languages spoken by the inhabitants of the lands they invaded. And aggressive of spirit they must have been. Despite the fact that they settled amiably enough among the farmer-hunters into whose fields and forests they drove their herds of half-wild cattle and horses, their thrill for combat came down to the Vikings undiluted. It is not certain, of course, that the Vikings are pure and direct descendants of the Battle-Ax people and the preceding settlers. But the Battle-Ax tomahawk of stone was once almost as common a find in Scandinavia as arrowheads are in America. Certainly the Vikings were by nature exactly like those who had laid the axes down.

Also knocking about Europe at approximately the same time, and certain to have visited even as far as the fjords, were those hardy rovers known as the Beaker Folk. Their fearlessness must have been matched only by their coolness and ability to get along with people. They were gypsy-like traders in bronze whose homeland was in Spain, where they must not have tarried very often. Their bell-beaker shaped pottery was found almost everywhere in Western Europe before archaeologists finally located the center from which they traveled out. It has been suggested that they peddled more than bronze. What they carried in their beaker pots may very well have been beer. Whether this was the reason they were accepted everywhere or not, archaeology records that after a while mixed communities of Battle-Ax and Beaker Folk appear even as far as England. Fragments of beaker pottery were found at Stonehenge and, by no coincidence, the Battle-Ax people were sun worshippers.

The weapon of the Beaker Folk was the bow. The pride they took in it is shown by the fact that in every male Beaker Folk grave there is a wrist guard, such as archers wear to protect their arms from the snap of

From The Testimony of the Spade, *by Geoffrey Bibby, 1956.*
Used by permission of Alfred A. Knopf, Inc.

BEAKER FOLK POTTERY

the bowstring. It is not likely that they introduced this weapon among the ancestors of the Vikings; the bow had been a hunter's tool for thousands of years. But they may very well have bequeathed the Vikings-to-be their enthusiasm for archery and their skill at it. Until the invention of the Pennsylvania rifle the bow was the most effective projectile weapon used by man.

The long sword of the Celts, the bow of the Beaker Folk, the assegai or javelin-spear of the Germanic tribes —all these the Vikings used with the hot-blooded zest of their Battle-Ax ancestors. But their long ships were entirely their own. Most prehistorians regard the Teutons or Germanic tribes as simply the non-seagoing branch of a single Nordic stock, and the Angles, Saxons, Danes as seagoing Nordics. Without these open-decked craft, built for speed and not for comfort, the Vikings would never have been anything but humble fisher folk and tillers of rocky farms. Driving their long ships across

25

the sullen North Sea and the moody Atlantic, they planted colonies in all the islands off Scotland, including the Shetlands and the Faroes; they peopled empty Iceland; and had they been as good historians as they were sailors they would now be known as the discoverers of America. They made landfalls here many times, probably as far south as Massachusetts.

They stole a whole province, the Dukedom of Normandy, from the Celts and Franks of France, and took Sicily in 1061. In 1066 when William, Duke of Normandy, wrested the throne of England from Harold the Saxon at Hastings, it was the second Norse invasion of England, and it has lasted ever since. Viking settlers in Greenland were the first permanent white inhabitants of the New World. Had not a bad turn of climate early in the 14th century ruined the Norse farms there, America might very well have been first colonized from Greenland ports. The Vikings were no people to sit-by-the-fire.

What the Viking long ships looked like, how they were made and what they were made of, there need be no guessing about. No perishable artifact or prehistory is better known than those oak-sided, pine-decked greyhounds of the sea. Some of them still exist. For they were buried whole and entire with the same loving and laborious care as the Viking royalty for whom they became the burial casket itself. Archaeologists have dug them up, and one at least was in such good condition that with a few days' repair it could have again put to sea.

3

Three Royal Ships

THERE SEEMS never to have been any doubt that the mound on a farm on the fjord of Oslo, in Norway, was the burial place of a king. Its local name was the King's Mound. According to local legend the royal treasure had also been buried there with the king. For all this juicy story, no owner of Gokstad, the farm on which the mound was located, had made any effort to open it. This despite the fact that the law at that time gave the owner full possession of any treasure he dug up. But perhaps there was more to the legend than was told abroad. Perhaps it had been handed down

The Viking ship from Gokstad

through the generations that the treasure had already been dug up.

It was shortly after the beginning of the year 1880 that Nikolas Nikolaysen, president of the Oslo Antiquarian Society, first heard about the King's Mound and the intention of its farmer-owner to get rich quick by digging it. To prevent the destruction of what might be valuable knowledge to archaeology, Nikolaysen, an experienced mound digger, volunteered his help and supervision.

It was well he did. By the end of the second day of shoveling Nikolaysen knew there lay under this mound that most incredible of finds, a thousand-year-old wooden ship still in almost perfect condition. He knew this so quickly because by then he had seen that the hull had been laid four feet deep in a bed of blue clay. Further, the ship had been packed inside, from stem to stern and gunwale to gunwale, with the same preservative. Over this had been laid a blanket of moss and over that a coverlet of hazel branches. Then tons of earth had been heaped over all. The King's ship could have lain safely thus another thousand years.

Here was no fragile relic, no mere shadow of what had been. The largest barge in Oslo harbor was just large enough to transport the King's ship from Gokstad to Oslo after Nikolaysen and his helpers had freed it. All that was missing were those sections of the prow, sternpost and mast that had projected out of the mound and into the weather. It was almost 80 feet long, displacing about 15 tons, and it had carried 32 oarsmen, 16 on each side. But rowing was not their sole or main occupation. At each oarport or opening was a circular war shield, three feet in diameter, the black and yellow paint of the design still menacingly visible. How many men and women had died before those shields, in what lands oversea, nobody knows. But these 32 warriors, hardened and muscled from plying their oars, must have taken their toll. Plainly, the only purpose for which this vessel had been built was piracy on the high seas and armed robbery on the land.

The Viking ship-carpenters knew how to build these hit-and-run raiders. For propulsion over open water the

King's ship carried a stepped mast; when the wind was running and the oarsmen rested, swiveled shutters covered the oarports. But in slack weather or close waters those 16 brawny oarsmen on a side must have given the craft the maneuverability of twin-screw power.

The sides or "skin" of the ship were of clinker construction. That is, the oaken planks overlapped each other, like the clapboards of a house. These had been tied with withes, not nailed to the frames, and the caulking was of three-strand rope of cattle-hair, laid in as the ship was built. It is evident that the Viking shipwrights were striving for elasticity, not rigidity. So these long ships must have moved through the buffeting waves with an almost muscular shift and "give," like living bodies. In fact, like the bodies of the sea serpents whose carved heads they carried at their prows.

The King's ship was a total working craft when Nikolaysen opened it to view. A gangplank and 32 oars were there, as well as the anchor stone, still on its hair-rope hawser. At the stern was the steering oar or tiller, and near it, as evidence of the far climes to which the ship had voyaged, were the bones and feathers of that royal bird, a peacock.

Yes, this blue-clay berth was the last port of call for the King's ship, but it was a vessel loaded for departure, not one emptied after a long cruise. There is no telling how rich this king was, but it would seem that all his personal wealth and all that could give him comfort in a Norway-like next world was stowed with him. His six dogs (one favorite had a collar of brass and another of iron) had been killed, to lie at his feet, and the diggers found bones of twelve horses. Perhaps half a dozen of these had been the King's own saddle mounts. But others must have been slain to become the draft animals, in spirit, that drew the sledge that had been packed aboard. Quite evidently the Vikings thought of the next world as having snowy winters.

The minute the King made a landfall in that next world he had what he needed to go ashore and set up camp. The ship carried a tent, with carved dragon-head tent poles, a copper kettle and an iron kettle with a tripod to hang them by over a cook fire, five bedsteads, and a plentiful supply of wooden cups, plates, bowls, barrels and kegs. Only a bolt of silk damask woven with a thread of gold through it was left of what must have been cloth enough to apparel the King for a long time after he had worn out the wardrobe he took with him. But this, judging from the buttons and buckles recovered, may well have included every stitch of clothing he had owned in life.

Nothing was lacking that the King might live forever after in kingly splendor and state. Trappings for his horses and several iron-bound chests had been placed in the special cabin that had been built on the ship to serve as his crypt or tomb. Here the King had been laid, with a leather purse handy and nearby a game board complete with draughtsmen to while away the hours of the long voyage.

Who was the King? He was a man of well over six feet, about fifty years old, who had been crippled by gout. His discovered bones told the anatomists that. But despite so much personal gear there was none by which he could be identified. Everything of precious metal, everything of value, everything that might have been impressed with the King's seal or his crest or his sign, had been stolen; Nikolaysen could be in no doubt about that. Along with everything else he found in the King's ship grave there were traces of the shaft the grave-robbers had dug into the burial chambers. It had happened, he saw, a very long time ago.

Yes, the King was dead, and he had been buried here with all his treasure. But who was the King and what had his treasure been?

Almost from the beginning, even before it was known that the ship buried at Oseberg was a Queen's, it was known that it, too, like the King's ship at Gokstad, had been looted. The digging of the mound had come about very much like that of the one at Gokstad, though some 24 years later. The tenant farmer at Oseberg had begun his own dig and had encountered what seemed to be the stump of a ship's mast. Prudently he had reported this to Professor Gabriel Gustafson, director of Oslo University's collection of Antiquities. Gustafson, who already had the King's ship in his charge and, aware that Oseberg was a scant 20 miles north of Gokstad, made every preparation for an important find.

Stern of the Oseberg ship showing Professor Gustafson

The Queen's ship was all of that. In itself it was smaller than the King's, about 71 feet long, displacing about 12 tons and carrying 30 oarsmen among its probable crew of 35. But archaeologically it was much richer, despite the looting.

Fourteen wooden spades and three litters for carrying away the spoils lay still scattered in the tunnel that ancient plunderers had dug the whole length of the ship. They had broken into the burial chamber from above, hacking through a beam that required 15 men to lift it.

Under the ship, when it was finally moved, were more wooden shovels, of the same style as those in the trench.

One can see, in fancy, this scene of pillage against the fog-thick night of a thousand years ago. The fog was there, certainly, for the Queen's ship was buried in what was then the only area of dry soil in the swampy lowlands within the reach of the tidewater of Oslo fjord. As a matter of fact, to reach its last anchorage, the ship must have been floated at high tide up a creek that passed nearby. In those days the farms were back in the uplands and on the slopes of higher ground. Looking down from their cottages at night, the peasants must have seen the torches of the robber band weaving eerily in and out of the steeping mists. To the children, at least, it must have been whispered that these were the lights of the trolls, the goblins who lived underground in Norwegian folklore.

But there must have been some who, looking down, shuddered for quite another reason. This was a formidable band of robbers. Fourteen shovels equal at least fourteen men. There must have been six or eight more to load out the dirt from the trench by litter and after that the booty. But we may assume that so much booty had to be carried across that marshland on something broader and better than men's backs. What better and likelier transport than a large boat or ship, rowed up that same creek by which the Queen's ship had come? So, while the digging goes on, a watch of perhaps two more men remains aboard this ship which has to be, as we now count up, large enough to carry a gang of about 25 men and all they have stolen. In fact, a ship as large, or almost as large, as the Queen's own ship. The countrymen back on the hills probably thought it best not to know too much or to spy too closely on what was being done at the burial mound. Anyway, how could they stop it?

But perhaps one of the pious farmers on the hill had seen too much and had gone for help. For there was evidence of haste in the robbers' departure scattered along the trench: the partial skeleton of a younger woman, probably a bondwoman or servant; woolen cloth, silk ribbons, and feathers from pillows and bedclothes; a wooden saddle; a carved dog's-head cane; a small cask of wild apples; wooden dishes, scoops and other utensils; and fragments of a loom.

Gustafson found that trench—in the exact condition the robbers had left it—all of a thousand years later, for it was decided that the ransacking had taken place not too long after the burial. One of the reasons for this conclusion was that the body of the Queen herself, lying in the trench, was missing its right hand, the fingers of the left hand and the upper left arm. Had there not been flesh on those members the robbers would not have had to cut them off, as they evidently did, to get at the jewelry they bore.

Even if the bones of the two women had never been found there could have been no doubt that a Queen had been laid in the burial chamber. Everything was rich

State sledge from the Oseberg ship

State carriage from the Oseberg ship

and plentiful, and it was all feminine: a large loom, combs, a thread box, a pair of scissors, a kitchen stool, hand milling stones, a frying pan, a pot-holder, awls, two iron lamps, figured cloth, a roll of tapestry——

The Queen had had her tent, too, and the cooking kettles and tripod and trenchers and all that was needed to prepare and consume her food. More than enough of that had been furnished her. There were chests of wheat and apples for her larder, and a young ox had been slain and put aboard for butchering. The King's ship had not been so well stocked as this. Perhaps it was thought that a man could better fend for himself.

There was nothing aboard that suggested a weapon, except two small hatchets used, probably, for splitting kindling for the kitchen fire, or for cutting meat. When Gustafson looked over the entire collection, after four months of digging, he reached a quick conclusion. The Queen's ship had been no war galley, but her personal vessel used for voyages of state, for visits to parts of her realm or to her far-flung estates. This was plain from the fact that among the ship's cargo were four sledges and a wheeled cart, all for land travel when the Queen disembarked. These carriages were beautifully carved, and though they had been smashed by the weight of earth and stone above them, when Gustafson brought them to light their paint was as brilliant as on the day of burial.

The Queen's ship, the sledges, the cart, all the lading of the Queen's last voyage, are on display in Oslo now.

It was all restored so that if the Queen were to return there today she would surely recognize her own property.

Since nothing identifiable was found in the two royal ships, there seemed small chance that the name of the King or the Queen or their place in the chronology of Norway would ever be known.

There was only one source of information to turn to, a story or chronicle called the Ynging Saga. It is like the *Iliad* in that it was long considered legend only, without historical basis. But when A. W. Brøgger, who succeeded Gustafson in his professorship (and who was one of the authors of the final report on the Queen's ship) consulted the Ynging Saga he came across a king of about A.D. 800–850 who had suffered from gout. This was the period of both the Gokstad and the Oseberg

The reconstructed Viking burial ship from Oseberg

burials, and soon everything began to fall into place.

According to the Ynging Saga there was once a king of a petty kingdom of western Norway whose beautiful young daughter Aasa was courted by King Gudrod of Vestfold. An elderly man and not blessed with many virtues, Gudrod was refused when he asked Aasa's hand in marriage. Whereupon, by a treacherous attack, he killed Aasa's father and brother and kidnapped the young princess. Though a son and heir, Halvdan, was born of this marriage, it could not have been happy. Within two years of the kidnapping, Gudrod was slain by a personal servant of Aasa's.

The kingdom fell jointly to the infant Halvdan, for whom Aasa probably reigned during his growing years, and to his half-brother, Olav, Gudrod's son by an earlier marriage. Halvdan was not yet old enough to marry when Olav died, leaving him the entire kingdom of Vestfold. (Olav is the king who was immobilized with gout and the Ynging Saga reports that he was buried in the district that now includes Gokstad.)

Halvdan seemed to have had his father's disposition. When he grew to manhood he, too, went forth and stole a bride, a lass called Ragnhild, though not necessarily against her will. No sooner had Ragnhild borne him a son than Aasa, now a grandmother, died at the age of fifty. (And fifty was the age, the anatomists had determined, of the elder woman of the two whose bodies were found at Oseberg.)

The story is not quite ended. Halvdan's son was

Harald Fairhair who united all Norway into one kingdom under himself and was its first fully historical ruler.

Archaeologists can ˙restore or reconstruct anything that has been left behind. But nowhere in Norway, Sweden or Denmark, which are the heart of the Viking land, has one long ship burial been found with all its treasure untouched. The Vikings took—and what they took was soon taken from them.

Only by sheerest accident did it seem possible that a ship burial's treasure would ever be found in place. (After all, the huge burial mounds, called barrows, with their freshly turned earth, must have advertised themselves like unguarded banks.) But that accident happened. When the ship barrow at Sutton Hoo, near the east coast of England, was excavated in 1939, everything was gone, including the ship—everything but the treasure.

The Sutton Hoo ship, at 89 feet, was the longest of the three buried ships, and the only one made with nails. None of its wooden frame remained, after some 1300 years in the sands of the tidal river Deben at the southeast coast of England. But the iron clench nails of its construction lay in the order in which they had fallen from the rotted hull. They outlined the shape perfectly, as the archaeologists delicately uncovered them with brushes, knives and needles. (Even trowels are too clumsy for this kind of work.)

All that was left of the Sutton Hoo ship were these nails and its impression in the sand. No one expected

The impression in the sand of the Sutton Hoo ship, with the original rivets in position, during the final stages of the excavation. The view is toward the stern.

much more when they saw that. Yes, the bones of him or her whose tomb this had been should be there, but anything not of metal would hardly have survived and metal was always the first thing taken by grave-robbers. A ship burial had been excavated in 1862 not ten miles from Sutton Hoo and it had been looted. Tombs will always be looted, be they of Egyptian Pharaohs or Norse nobility. Nobody was surprised when it was discovered that grave-robbers had indeed sunk a shaft into the Sutton Hoo mound.

Yet nothing about the Sutton Hoo ship was what it seemed. The ship was there, but it wasn't, really. There was only its image in the sand, outlined in rusty nails. Nor had any body been buried there. Not a scrap of bone was found. Chemical tests of the soil were run for dissolved bone, to no avail. What was there, having been completely missed by the grave-robbers, who had stopped their trench too soon, was the treasure.

Now, for the first time, archaeologists had more than an inkling of what genuine wealth must have been buried with Viking royalty. Treasure trove does not come with price tags on it, so there is no standard for fixing its worth. Beyond the precious-metal value of the gold and silver of the Sutton Hoo treasure is the value that must be added because it consists of objects of art, of the gold- and silversmith's craft. And beyond that is the incalculable value of its age and rarity. C. W. Phillips, who conducted the Sutton Hoo dig, estimated the treasure's worth at "a very substantial six-figure sum," that is, several hundred thousands. Being English, Mr. Phillips was talking not about hundreds of thousands of dollars, but pounds. The pound was then worth about $2.90. A million dollars would probably not buy the treasure.

The courts awarded the whole of it to the owner of the land where the Sutton Hoo barrow or mound lay. A Mrs. E. M. Pretty by name, she lived up to it fully. Once title was determined she presented the treasure to the British government.

Despite the absence of the body of him in whose honor the ship had been buried, there was no doubt from the beginning that he was a personage of power, probably royalty. Among the first objects found was a two-foot-long ceremonial whetstone. Since this had a swordlike blade, a knob carved into a crown at the top and four grim faces carved just beneath this, most authorities now agree that it was probably a scepter. Found with it was an iron standard, perhaps for flying a flag or pennant.

The chief finds at Sutton Hoo, and not duplicated at Gokstad or Oseberg, were these: a bronze and iron helmet that looks very much like a football helmet, with face mask or protector; sword and shield, with the jeweled fittings of the sword belt; a set of seven assorted spears with a dirk or dagger; jeweled epaulettes, or shoulder pieces, from a cuirass or body armor; a bronze bowl containing a hanging bowl which in turn contained the remains of a harp; a set of ten matched silver bowls from the Near East; two silver spoons, one with the name of Paul, the other with the name of Saul, in Greek letters;

Iron and bronze helmet from the Sutton Hoo ship-burial

a collection of drinking horns (two of these would hold six quarts each) with silver mountings; a small silver dish; a coat of mail; three great bronze cauldrons; and finally a purse of 37 gold coins from France. This was the most valuable single hoard uncovered to date in English archaeology.

Its value to knowledge was, as we are now aware from the Gokstad and Oseberg burials, as great as its monetary value. By means of the French coins the Sutton Hoo

burial was dated at no later than A.D. 650, after the fall
of the Roman Empire. At this time, we learn from a
history written by St. Bede in A.D. 731, this was the kingdom of East Anglia. Its rulers were related to the royal
family of Uppland, in Sweden, and they had a royal
residence at a place called Rendlesham. As of now there
is a little village called Rendlesham within four miles of
Sutton Hoo.

He who was not in his own tomb may very well have
been a son of, or the successor to Raedwald, King of East
Anglia, who claimed the title of Overlord of Britain and
who died about A.D. 625. Why was the body not in the
tomb? It has been guessed that this royal or noble personage was lost at sea, or was killed in battle and his
body fell to the enemy. Or, again, it is possible that he

Gold belt-buckle, 5⅞" in length, from the Sutton Hoo ship-burial

was a Christian and was buried elsewhere, in consecrated ground. Ship burial is a pagan rite and prepares the departing soul not for heaven but for Valhalla. This, then, is the strangest thing of all about the richest ship burial known—it was but a cenotaph, a monument to a man of prehistory whose name, though it must have been great and powerful once, we shall probably never know.

Yet we have gained much in knowledge. This kingdom of East Anglia had been conquered by the Germanic tribe of Angles from the west Germanic district of Seinswick more than 200 years before the birth of Aasa and Gudrod. They had come in long ships and somewhere along the line had become related to the Vikings of Sweden. They were to remain longer in possession of their English realms than the United States has been a nation, before a new invasion of long ships would strike them. The new blood, new laws, new ways came to England as the Norse and Danish Vikings went out into the world to seek their fortunes, and found the Angles and Saxons easy picking.

And what of the once rampaging Celts? They were ancient history; or rather prehistory, in this part of England at the time of the Sutton Hoo ship burial. But they were there. The beautiful craftsmanship in some of the gold and silver treasure was Celtic. It was the same craftsmanship that had enabled the Celts of a thousand years before to forge the iron long swords that made them the lords of the continent.

4

The Ice Age Is
Still with Us

MOST OF US are accustomed to a life of routine.
We follow the same streets or roads to school and
to work every day. Along the way and from our windows
at home we see the same landscapes and horizons. We
note that whatever changes take place in the world about
us are man-made, whether it be a building going up,
or a tearing down by bulldozer or bomb. We tend to
think, therefore, of the earth itself as being solidly inert,
in a state more or less fixed for as long as it will last.

Oh yes, we read that there was a time when great
mountains of ice stood where there are now populous

nations, including our own. And the oceans had a habit of getting out of hand. But that was long ago, wasn't it, during the earth's wild youth? It has settled down since then, to a quiet and stable maturity, hasn't it?

A simple "no" is not really negative enough. If the current warming trend in climate continues, within the next few thousand years, give or take a few centuries, New York City—that is, what we now think of as the population and cultural center of the Western World—will be under water. The archaeologists of A.D. 100,000 will be descending, probably in diving bells, to recover artifacts such as typewriters and department store dummies from Fifth Avenue offices and shops 100 feet beneath the open Atlantic.

The truth of the matter is that we are still living in an ice age. There is still enough frozen water in the ice caps to drown all the great coastal cities of the world when it melts. The geologist Rhodes W. Fairbridge has calculated that at its greatest extent the last glacier consisted of about 56,000,000 cubic miles of ice. Of this about half is still left. While the now melted half was melting, the level of the sea rose 320 feet. In time the remaining half will melt, without doubt. During most of its geologically known career the earth has had no polar ice, nor any amount of permanent ice at all except, probably, on mountain peaks.

How fast this melting will proceed is a matter of the moods of climate. Despite all the talk of oldsters, the present climate is rather well balanced. Sea level at New

York is rising about 4 millimeters a year. At that, 3 mm. are due to a sinking of the coast and only 1.2 mm. to actual water rise all over the world as a measure of the melting of polar ice.

But actually sea level had only been oscillating, reflecting minor climate changes, a few feet above or a few feet below the present level over the last 6,000 years. Before that things were quite different. From about 15,000 till 6,000 years ago there was a general retreat from the last Great Ice Age. As melt water from the shrinking glaciers poured into the ocean, the sea level rose at the phenomenal rate, for decades on end, of 3 or 4 inches a year. The rise was at such a startling rate from about 6000 years ago to 5800 years ago, that Fairbridge thinks it is the origin of the tradition, found among many ancient peoples and in the Bible, about a deluge or great flood that once inundated the earth.

A man who lived a modest lifetime of 60 years during this period would have seen the ocean rise 16 feet. If he lived on the coast or along a tidal river such as the Hudson, many of the landmarks of his boyhood would have disappeared, under 8 feet of water, by the time he was 30. His grandchildren would probably think he was out of his head when he told them how the world had looked when he was young, and that he had once gathered berries from bushes long since submerged.

This time of high water lasted, according to the calculations of Fairbridge and other scientists, until about 4500 years ago. There were three phases of rise and fall

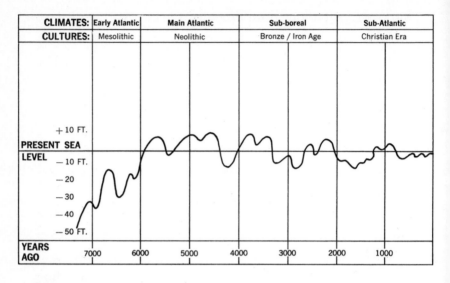

CLIMATES:	Early Atlantic	Main Atlantic	Sub-boreal	Sub-Atlantic
CULTURES:	Mesolithic	Neolithic	Bronze / Iron Age	Christian Era

The rise and fall of sea level during the past 7,000 years (*based after Rhodes W. Fairbridge*).

over this span of 1500 years, with water level falling during cold periods and rising again during warm periods. Cold weather causes water to be withdrawn from the sea and to be stored in glaciers; warm weather releases this stored water into the sea again by melting the glacial ice. Fairbridge has found that these warm and cold spells come and go in a sort of rhythm, in spells about 550 years long. But it was not until 4500 years ago that there came a spell cold enough to drop sea level below the level it is now.

Then, after a 550 year interval, the sea began to swell again, from about 10 feet below to another 10-12 feet above present level. This was not quite as spectacularly sudden a rise as that of 6000 years ago, but it was fast enough to drown whole forests along the sea coast. One drowned forest from this period can be found today at Throggs Neck, the Bronx, New York—if you are a skindiver.

After some 500 years of warmth, the long hard winters came back and, from all sea level indications, continued colder than at present until 2600 years ago, when a warm spell brought sea level up to 4 feet above present level during the next hundred years. There had been a brief rise about 400 years earlier, but it did not reach present or what we call normal level.

If we regard today's sea level and climate as the norm —that is, the average of the fluctuations or changes of the past 6000 years—we will come quickly to an appreciation of what these fluctuations mean. A rise of two or three degrees in weather average would give New England a climate like that of New Jersey, whereas an equal drop would return it to that situation which caused somebody to remark, a hundred years ago, that Maine had but two seasons, winter and July. The money that would be saved and earned by warmth would run into millions annually: less fuel would be required for homes, stores and plants; there would be less snow to plow and less winter damage to roads and other installations; there would be more working days outdoors and a longer growing season; real estate values would increase and the tourist and resort business would be much more bustling. Heat, to some extent, is a priceless economic asset.

Archaeology has probed into many sites where the

shifts of climate have cut their mark, but none shows more clearly the cycle of climate during the last 4000 years, as it has just been outlined from Fairbridge, than the little village of Jarlshof, in the Shetland Islands.

In the first place, Jarlshof is at almost exactly the same latitude, 60°N, as the southern tip of Greenland, which the Vikings once settled during a warm climatic phase and had to give up during a cold one. Though the Shetlands are in the northeastern Atlantic and somewhat favored by the warm Gulf Stream, they are still some 100 miles north of Scotland, very decidedly in a marginal climatic zone. A slight change in weather average can make them pleasantly habitable, or a place of bare existence.

In the second place, all those who settled at Jarlshof during the 4000 years of its up-and-down existence were farmers, and farming is very sensitive to changes of weather. The hunter light-heartedly follows his game as it migrates to greener pastures, but the farmer must stick to the fields he has planted and take what the heavens send. Two or three bad crops in a row and he is in serious trouble. When the climate turns against him, his fate has been written if he cannot leave for a better land. At Jarlshof it was written, as we shall see, in the sands.

But the importance of Jarlshof, called by its latest and most thorough excavator, J. R. C. Hamilton, "one of the most remarkable archaeological sites ever excavated in northwest Europe," is more than simply as an index of climatic change. With each climatic change for the better, a new group of settlers sought out Jarlshof. Each group of settlers brought with it whatever advances had been made or adopted in the living ways of men in the lands from which they came. The first settlers did not have the use of metal; the next group brought bronze; then came men of the early and late iron age; finally there came the Vikings. What Jarlshof is, then, is a short form of an illustrated lecture on the prehistory of Europe from the Stone Age to historic times. It certainly bears digging into.

5

A Popular Place with Viking Raiders

IT MUST HAVE BEEN more than coincidence that the Vikings began their overseas venturing about A.D. 800 at just that time when the climate had turned mild again, after seven or eight centuries of severity. Returning warmth meant higher sea level, and higher sea level meant the invasion by water of some of their precious little farmland, along the narrow fjord valleys. From the position inland of the Gokstad and Oseberg ship burials we already know that the sea must have been higher at that time than now. Need of living room as well as a love of adventure stimulated the Vikings.

The archaeologist Hamilton thinks that the Vikings must have occupied the Shetlands no later than A.D. 800. Every argument is in his favor.

Jarlshof is on Sumburgh Bay. Over it towers Sumburgh Head, straight out of the sea to a height of 928 feet. A Viking pilot, having brought his long ship through the Skagerrak that separates Norway and Denmark, and having watched the coast of Norway drop behind him as he sailed west, must have moved immediately to a forward lookout station and waited for the loom of Sumburgh Head to starboard. In clear weather the wait would not have been long. Sumburgh Head is but some 120 miles off the Norwegian coast.

Any old salt could tell what the pilot did. He held a course on Sumburgh Head that would take him south of it, to the next landfall, Fair Island, which is some 700 feet high. But he kept his eye on the weather and if it began to dirty a bit, he changed course to northwest and headed for the safe harbor of Sumburgh Bay. Many a Viking long ship must have sat out many a North Sea squall in that haven, for this was the raiders' route to western Scotland, the Hebrides and Ireland. Since the Irish monasteries were raided by Vikings as early as A.D. 793, Hamilton's belief that Jarlshof was settled about A.D. 800 in every way holds water. In his excavations he even found trinkets taken in raids on Ireland and probably given to the lady of the house at the Viking farmstead of Jarlshof in appreciation of her hospitality. Or, even more likely, they were given to the daughter of the house by some young bravo of a Viking for the usual reason—to impress her.

At any rate, both coming and going, Sumburgh Bay was a popular place with Viking raiders. Any place so well known and so near to Scandinavia had to be one of the first places settled when Viking farmers went looking for new fields and homesteads. Those who happened upon it first, coming in two or three craft loaded with livestock, household furnishings and family, must have been mildly astonished to find so liveable a place so available.

Here were fine springs of fresh water, good pasturage, fields on the slopes of Sumburgh Head level enough to be tillable, plenty of stone and driftwood for building (the area is treeless), and all this on the shores of a snug harbor and fishing grounds that seemed to be an inexhaustible cupboard.

In possession of all this were only a few listless local inhabitants who could have put up little resistance. If they put up any resistance at all it was not to the death. In his excavations Hamilton turned up a building which proved to be a sort of bunkhouse where these erstwhile owners of Jarlshof were sheltered, having docilely become the thralls, that is, servants and farmhands to the new Viking owners.

It would add a good deal to our story if we knew whether the Vikings ever asked their servants why Jarlshof was so available. Surely these natives, whose ancestry at this spot went back perhaps a thousand years, could have told them what had happened to the thriving little settlement their forefathers had once built here. Perhaps keeping silent was their idea of revenge upon the Vikings for having taken their lands. It takes very little imagination to picture an old native Jarlshofian grandmother sitting in the newly built bunkhouse and saying to the clan gathered about her, "Why should we tell these invaders anything? Let them find out for themselves. Sooner or later IT will get them, too."

What was IT that would get the Vikings, too?

The sands. The very choking, overwhelming sands under which lay buried all the villages that had been built at Jarlshof since the first one in 2000 B.C. And it is not getting too far ahead of our story to say that the sands did get the Viking village. The archaeologist Hamilton who dug the Viking settlement out of the sands reports, "A decline in the settlement took place about the end of the 13th century."

This alone should give us all the clue we need to understand the attacks of the enemy sands at Jarlshof. It was at the beginning of the 14th century that the climate had turned so difficult in Greenland that the Vikings there could no longer successfully raise cattle, their main support. Now, sand has no legs, nor power to move itself; therefore, if it swept up from the beaches to smother the houses of Jarlshof, it must have been driven. Storm-driven. But these must have been "unusual" storms. The sands of the "usual" seasonal storms could be coped with by sweeping and cleaning. But a series of "unusual" storms, during the kind of weather that occurs when the climate turns bad, can very soon erase the works of man, kill his stock and make sterile his fields. Joined with shorter summers and longer, colder winters the storms came again and again to kill off a Jarlshof settlement, on a schedule we already know. It was the schedule charted by Fairbridge for the rise and fall of the sea, for the melting and the remaking of glacial ice.

But the Viking settlers who took their families and livestock ashore in A.D. 800 had some 500 years of good weather ahead of them. They built cheerfully and stoutly for this half a thousand years of peace and comparative plenty. The first thing that must be said about these Vikings was that they were not of the bloodthirsty disposition of their raiding kinfolk. A single spearhead was the only weapon recovered by the excavators. There were no long swords or shields or arrowheads. This lack of evidence would indicate that these settlers did not even hunt. They were simple farmers, or probably it is better to say they were ranchers, in a country where there was neither human nor animal foe.

The Vikings raised hay and grain, but principally they raised pigs, sheep, cattle, and the ponies by which the Shetlands are known to us. We would have no difficulty recognizing this layout as a ranch. The main house was a comfortable, one-story structure 70 feet long, of stone and wood brought from the homeland. It was divided into two large rooms, a kitchen and a living room. Close by, within a stone wall enclosure that had been built by the pre-Viking settlers, there was erected a stock barn, a hay barn, a blacksmith's shop, the bunkhouse, and a small building that may have been a hof, or family chapel, for worship.

Within 50 or 60 years a second farmstead or ranch house was built near the first, indicating an increase in population, which in turn indicated that the little settlement was prospering and its inhabitants were content with their lives. If they had not been they could quite easily have returned to Norway with raider ships going home, or they could have moved elsewhere in the Shetlands which the Norse were now taking over in considerable numbers. Within another generation and a half, about a century after the first Viking landing, a third farmstead was built. Peace and plenty—this was what Jarlshof had to offer when the climate was in a smiling mood.

Yet by the 12th century something has begun to happen. The Jarlshofians are no longer farmer-ranchers. They keep some livestock, they raise a little grain, but they have become principally fishermen. The new dwellings which have been recently erected are much smaller than the original ranch houses—it is easier to heat smaller houses—and the tool or artifact most often found is a stone fishing-line weight. What can be assumed but that the conditions which had made the Jarlshof locale so satisfactory to husbandmen had begun to break down? To fill out their diet, to provide three meals a day for the population, it was necessary to find another source of staple food. Fortunately there was one —the fishing grounds of Sumburgh Bay.

Now the year no longer followed the calendar of the old Norse farmer-rancher, which ran thus:

Gaukmanuor—cuckoo month, the time of the mating and nesting of the boisterous cuckoo.

Saotid—seed or planting month.

Eggtid or Stekktid—egg month and lambing month, when the eggs of wild fowl could be collected for food and lambs and calves were dropped.

Selmanour—the pasture or dairy month when cows, recently fresh with the dropping of their calves, fed on the lush spring grass and gave the most milk.

Heyannir—the haying month, when hay was cut and stacked.

Kornskuoramanuor—the month of the harvest of "corn" (to Europeans corn means the grain crops, barley, wheat).

Gormanuor—the butchering month, when the cattle, sheep and pigs marked for winter meat were killed and smoked or salted down.

Frermanuor, Thorri, Goi, Einmanuor and Morsugur (the "fat-sucking" mid-winter months of feasts)—the shut-in months of cold, of keeping up the fires, of mending gear and preparation for the new year in the fields.

Now the seasons were the seasons of the sea, counted by the spawning runs and feeding movement of fish. Hamilton has summed up this change by pointing out that since that time the Orkneymen (from the Orkney

Islands, some 70 miles to the south and that much better off climatically) have been known as crofters with a boat; that is, farmers who fish on the side. But the Shetlanders have become fishermen with a croft; that is, fishermen who farm on the side.

This has been so since, in Hamilton's words, there was a decline in the settlement about the end of the 13th century.

But all this—a time of comfortable farming, then of reliance on the sea, then of the coming of the sands— had happened at Jarlshof before. Many times before.

6

Stone Age Farmers

U P TO NOW the two terms "archaeology" and "prehistory" have been used as though they had about
the same meaning. In that they deal with the same
material, they have. It is in the direction of movement
that they differ. Prehistory, like history, follows the nar-
rative sequence of human events, from the earliest traces
of man until he begins to set down his deeds in writing.
The method of archaeology is the reverse of this. The
archaeologist begins at the surface, at the level of now,
and spades his way down and thus backward in time.

It is as archaeologists that we shall proceed with our

investigations of what was under the sands that the
Vikings built their ranch houses on so firmly, and of who
were the people they turned so readily to their service.

The people, to begin with, were of a mixed and most
interesting ancestry. One strain traced back to early Iron
Age settlers who had seated themselves at Jarlshof perhaps 500 years B.C. Some of them had survived the cold
spell that began slightly before A.D. 1 and piled up two
to three feet of sand over their round huts. Among these
had come the mysterious builders of what is known
throughout this part of the world as a broch tower.

There are two theories about the building of broch
towers. One is that these businesslike fortresses were
built by the natives against a threatened invader. But
there is little or no evidence that such a threat ever developed into any real danger, although over 500 broch
towers have been found throughout northern Scotland
and the islands nearby. Hence the second theory seems
the more likely. It is that small bands of warlike men
scattered throughout this part of the world, including
Jarlshof, and set themselves up as overlords, using the
broch towers as castle keeps. The Norman conquerors
of England set up such keeps after A.D. 1066 to protect
themselves from the hostile Saxon population.

They are fascinating structures, these brochs, and certainly designed for living in during long periods of
defense. They would not have held as large a defending
force as the log forts into which the pioneers retreated
during Indian attack, but they were not nearly so vul-

nerable. Built of stone, they would not burn, and nothing but cannon, which would not be invented for a thousand years, could have broken into them.

The base of a broch was of solid stone about 12 to 18 feet thick which enclosed an open courtyard. On this base wall were built two separate walls—an outer wall, and an inner one overlooking the courtyard. In the space between these two walls a stairway ascended, leading to rooms or galleries. From these rooms the defense could be conducted, through slit windows in the outer walls, or wider window-like openings, which also admitted light.

The living quarters were in rooms on the ground level, opening on the courtyard. This was entered from outside the tower through a single gateway flanked by two guard rooms. Altogether the tower rose 30 to 40 feet above ground and gave its inmates great advantage as a lookout station, as well as a tight fortification.

The evidence that men and women had lived here was scant, but present. There were bone dice—with which soldiers have whiled away their time and lost their pay as long as there have been soldiers—and weaving combs, and pottery. This pottery is the only clue to who the broch tower overlords were. They seem to have been a small band of invaders from the Orkneys and they had not actually built the tower. They had conscripted the local residents for the work.

It was not long in use. There is nothing at all to show that the local residents rose in revolt and captured it.

But indeed, if this is what did happen there would probably be no sign of it. Almost certainly the tower could have been taken not by assault but only by treachery from within or by some strategem that would have left no marks. Perhaps the garrison was starved out, or left of its own accord, or simply intermarried with the local girls. A life of watching out over the black sea and the empty mists off the moors for an enemy that never comes is not very exciting or rewarding or comfortable. And who knows? Perhaps somebody forgot to pay the broch tower men-at-arms and they simply quit.

At any rate the native Jarlshofians did not seem to have feared reprisal. As soon as the tower had been quitted they began to tear it down, to build a large wheelhouse at its base. This type of house had distinct advantages for this section of the world because it was the easiest to heat with a single, center fire. Where fuel is scarce, as in the treeless Shetlands, and that fuel is peat which does not burn hotly, and the winters are long, house design can mean the difference between life and death.

Now there came to Jarlshof about the third century A.D. a real invasion from the south, a peaceable and an advantageous one. The natives had been eking out their living by a combination of farming, ranching, fishing and seal hunting. The newcomers brought with them advanced methods of farming, and the fact that they immediately laid out the fields in a new and better plan

Iron-Age wheelhouses, seen from the top of the broch.

seems to prove that they immediately took control of the
Sumburgh district.

The Fairbridge chart on sea level shows these immigrants to have come to Jarlshof during a time of low
water, hence unfavorable climate. What happens, then,
to the case we have been building up for the popularity
of Jarlshof during warm periods and its waning during
cold periods?

Nothing very serious, we hope. We are dealing here

with people, and sometimes they flee from conditions more intolerable to them than merely severe climate. The method of separating the grain from the stalk with a notched slate stick—which these latest immigrants brought with them—was the same method in vogue in southwest Britain. Here were living at this time Celtic tribes more or less sullen under the overlordship of their Roman conquerors.

Not content with what they had, the Romans kept pushing northward to subdue Scotland, a project they were never quite able to accomplish. Whenever the legions moved out in force on one of these Scotching campaigns the tribes in their rear took advantage of the temporary Roman weakness and rebelled. The glamorous, golden-haired warrior Queen Boadicea led one such rebellion of her people, and the punishment was terrible. Her lands did not recover for generations.

From these circumstances we can create a picture of Roman-harassed farmers taking to boats and probing along the west coast of Britain for a site unoccupied and suitable for the start of a new community. Not until they have traversed to what must have been to them the northern rim of the world, to the Shetlands, do they find that place. It must have looked as wonderful and heaven-sent to them as Massachusetts looked to the Pilgrims or Pennsylvania to the Quakers 1300 years later when they, too, fled a no longer friendly homeland.

These new immigrants set to the development of this land of their adoption with such vigor that they brought

Jarlshof to what was probably its most populous stage. The broch tower was further dismantled for building stone for new wheel houses, and as late as A.D. 500 the village was being expanded.

For at least two centuries, perhaps a little longer, these late Iron Age farmers held their own against the longest cool climatic spell in the last 6000 years. We know now that these Jarlshofians had two centuries of harsh weather and what archaeologist Hamilton called "the ever-mounding sand" ahead of them. The settlement began to wane. "During the final post-broch phase," Hamilton says, "only a few scattered families inhabited the site, living in earth houses and small huts." These "few scattered families" were those whom the Vikings met as they stepped ashore.

And this, as we shall see when we dig down through more layers of sand drift, is the story, ever repeated, of Jarlshof. The good times are always at the beginning. Nothing is ever accomplished which surpasses the beginning, and the end is always in defeat.

Having stripped away the sand layer from the Viking settlement, and from the two phases of the late Iron Age —the progressive farmers and the broch tower occupants —we find under the foundations of the broch tower the wheel or beehive houses of an early Iron Age village.

These Early Iron Age beehives differed from the round houses only in the attachment of a souterrain, an underground chamber connected with the house by a walled passage. However romantic it might be to imagine these as dungeons, any American farmer of 50 years ago would have recognized them instantly and called them root cellars. They were storage rooms for the winter food supply and their presence marks their builders as prudent farmers who knew what winter was.

These farmers were also from Britain, but from the east and south rather than the southwest. The kind of pottery they made has been found near Scarborough, a seacoast town in Yorkshire, on the sites of Iron Age or Hallstatt people of about 2500 years ago. Now, pottery is to the archaeologist what fingerprints are to the detective. Just as files of fingerprints are kept for comparison and identification, so pot sherds are "filed" away in archaeological keeping and thus all the main pottery-making traditions in western Europe are very well known. That these sherds of the Early Iron Age settlers made pottery referrable to Hallstatt opens a whole treasure chest . . . For with Hallstatt we are back among the Celts.

The Celts, as we already know, came to Britain in two different waves. The first arrivals reached the island about the 6th century B.C., and carried swords of bronze. This was in the very last days of the Bronze Age. A hundred years later, Celtic migration continuing, they were bearing swords and daggers of iron. With these weapons, and their skill and readiness at using them, they had no difficulty making room for themselves among the farmers and surviving Stone Age hunters of Britain.

These Celts are called Hallstatt because this period of transition from bronze to iron is found in the famous Celtic cemetery at Hallstatt, in Austria.

From The Testimony of the Spade, *by Geoffrey Bibby, 1956.*
Used by permission of Alfred A. Knopf, Inc.

A bronze brooch with chain pendants from Austria, of the time of the Hallstatt Cemetery.

Hallstatt pottery at Jarlshof does not necessarily mean, though, that the settlers there were of this original Hallstatt Celtic British immigrant stock. They may very well have been Hallstatt Celts who had lived long enough in Britain to have become natives and who were themselves disturbed by another wave of Celts called La Tène.

These were the tribesmen of the Celtic Golden Age amongst whose exploits was the sacking of Rome in 390 B.C. They had already spread themselves over western Europe and for the next four centuries were to leave their mound graves, their distinctive art and their tribal names all over the landscape. (Paris, for instance, is named from the Celtic tribe of the Parisi.)

The mound graves are thickest along the Rhine and the Marne rivers and they are not so different, in the essentials, from the Viking ship burials. It was the Celtic chieftain's war chariot, in the place of a long ship, that went into the grave, along with his horses or, more usually, their harness and trappings. Restlessness, recklessness, vanity and a sure sense of the artistic—these are the traits of the La Tène Celts we find in their grave goods. The warriors carried bronze-handled, iron-bladed dirks and swords, wooden shields ornamented with bronze mountings, and sometimes helmets of metal. But more often they went into battle bareheaded, so vain were they about their hair. They wore long cloaks fastened at the shoulder with jeweled safety pins and their arms were likely to be covered with all manner of personal jewelry. Our good earth may never again see such a combination of warrior and artist as these dashing Celts of La Tène.

Usually in their graves there is found, stuck in the mouth of a pot or vase, a pig ham. The La Tène Celts were the only warrior people to raise the pig to the status of an heroic or symbolic animal. This was not necessarily because they loved pork. The porcine beast they exalted was the wild boar, which they hunted as the English came to hunt foxes, or Americans to hunt deer or bear. As quarry the wild boar is more dangerous than any bear except the grizzly or Kodiak bear and very nearly as dangerous as the sladang or wild buffalo of the Far East.

It was, apparently, to seize control of the metal trade that these boar-hunting cutthroat La Tène Celts invaded Britain. The Hallstatt Celts, their older cousins, by now true Britons, prepared to defend themselves by fortifying their homesteads or a nearby hilltop with ditch and bank, or ramparts of stone and timber. In some instances the La Tène invaders were driven off. In many they were not and often enough the onslaught came so suddenly that fortifications were not even finished. But the conclusion was foregone. In the end the La Tène Celts became the overlords of what is now England.

It is entirely plausible that the Hallstatt pottery makers at Jarlshof had been dispossessed or crowded out of their lands during La Tène times and brought their old ways with them. One observation about these and all other Jarlshof settlers ought to be made. They must all have been farmers along tidal rivers on the seacoast. Otherwise it would not have occurred to them to migrate overseas. Their settling at Jarlshof, on the shores of Sumburgh Bay, rather than farther inland, confirms that they were accustomed to and preferred coastal locations. It was this preference which was their undoing, when the sands came. The broch tower builders, it will be recalled, had two to three feet of it on which to lay their foundation stones when they followed the Hallstatt pottery makers.

When we consult the Fairbridge chart on the ups and

downs of sea level we find a 4-foot peak at about 2700 years ago, with good climate lasting only a few centuries. There is then a short, sharp drop to present sea level and an almost immediate rebound upward at about 2400 years ago, which is the time of the occupation of Jarlshof by the Hallstatt pottery makers. When we dig beneath the occupation level of these Early Iron Age people, we expect to find Bronze Age people. And we expect to find that they date at about the time of the 4-foot peak of 2700 years ago.

We are not disappointed. Not only is there a Jarlshof village of late Bronze Age farmers buried in the sand, but it had its own bronze-smith. His broken casting molds are found plentifully in the abandoned hut where he set up his shop.

The archaeologist Hamilton thinks this bronze-smith was, perhaps, an Irishman shipwrecked at Jarlshof where there was scarcely enough wealth or business to make him rich. On the other hand he may merely have been looking for a place where his bronze-casting skill had some value. The age of iron was coming in, in the more advanced regions, and the trade of bronze-smithing was going out.

Our Irish smith must have brought a supply of Cornwall tin with him, but there was plenty of copper only 12 miles north of Jarlshof. He was an industrious man, whatever his prospects were, and he made the whole gamut of bronze tools—swords, axes, pins, gouges. That he disposed of them remains questionable. He may very well have been the first business failure we know of in prehistory.

The Jarlshof to which he had come was well along in its career; probably it was already in decline, which accounts for the little difference he made in its ways. But it had been for a while a comfortable little hamlet of houses built on a slightly different plan from the bee-hives of the Iron Agers. The early houses, though radially divided like the wheel houses, were oval, and one section was set aside for the stabling of a cow or cows. In one house a whalebone tether ring was found fastened to a wall and the stone floor had been sloped for the removal of the dung. Undoubtedly this was used as manure, the earliest record anywhere of the intentional use of organic fertilizer.

Cattle keeping in the family habitation is not as sloven a practice as it might seem offhand. Any old farmer would guess that it was a milch cow which was given this special protection. Exposure to severe weather dries up a milker in no time, whereas good care not only keeps up the supply but the cream content as well. As might be supposed, these Bronze Age Jarlshofians were cattle-men first, yet their solicitude for cattle dung and the layout of their farmsteads show that they were almost equally farmers.

Their oval huts were set in the midst of a tilled plot of ground which was surrounded by a stone wall. Obviously this wall fenced the cattle out of the "corn," that is, the millet, barley and emer wheat. This kind of farmstead was already an old tradition in the British Isles and where to look for the port of embarkation of the Jarlshof Bronze Agers is a matter of wide choice. The pottery, too, is traceable down through the Orkneys, into Scotland and England. But it had come, in the beginning, from farther away than that, from across the North Sea and the English Channel, out of the Low Countries of the continent.

In this movement of Bronze Age people we are very likely dealing with one of the best-known weather breaks in prehistory. Shortly before 2700 B.C. a sharp climatic change forced the abandonment of the famous Swiss villages built on piles either out in lakes or on marshy ground on their shores. Not only is there argument about whether these villages were in the lake or on the swampy shore, but about what caused the lakes to rise and force their abandonment. Some authorities take it for granted that the lakes flooded during a spell of cold, rainy weather. Others say the opposite, that a spell of hot weather brought spates of melt water down from the mountain glaciers into the lakes. A glance at the Fairbridge chart does not help us much. Fifty years one way or the other and the cause could have been either cold weather or hot, though the chances seem best that it was hot.

The cause could not have concerned the villagers very much; the high lake levels forced them to move. It is probable that a good many other peoples had to make some adjustments also. By this time husbandry had been practiced in western and northern Europe at least 1500 years and it is the most notable benefit of husbandry that it can feed a great many more mouths than any other method of food getting. Every prolonged spell of good weather brings farming prosperity and population increase. Every harmful turn of weather brings disturbance to more and more people. Whatever "unusual" weather occurred about 2700 years ago, it sent a good many farmers on the move for better living conditions. It even had its effect on far-off Jarlshof.

The Bronze Age occupation of Jarlshof was probably the shortest, before the blight of sands overtook it. The occupation under it, the first in point of time but the last, to us as digging archaeologists, was probably the longest. About 4000 years ago, on the Fairbridge chart, the earth entered an almost exuberant spell of fine climate that lasted at least 600 years and coincided, at its beginning, with the beginnings of husbandry in northern and western Europe. The prehistory of the time seems to reflect the climatic high spirits. Everybody seemed to be going somewhere. It is not at all strange that during this period a people found Sumburgh Bay and Jarlshof.

Here again we are confronted with migrants who may have been in flight, but who certainly went searching for new lands during a fortunate time, when a climatic high had made new land available in the north. About 3650 years ago a mixed Battle-Ax Beaker-Folk people, having crossed from the Low Countries, had taken over in south and central England and in eastern Scotland. They brought with them aristocratic ideas about a division of society into ruling classes and lower classes. Of course they cast themselves in the role of the ruling class. The native population of Stone Age farmers and hunters became the ruled.

The first settlers, the founders of Jarlshof, we know by their possessions to have been of the lower, farming class. They brought no battle-axes with them, no beakers and, above all, no bronze. The first Jarlshofians were still Stone Age people, although in the last age of stone.

The oval houses they built were very much the same radially divided basic type we have known all through the Jarlshof occupation, up to the Vikings' rectangular ranch house. Excavation has uncovered some 30 feet of the stone fence that enclosed one of the farm plots, in the same kind of layout used by the Bronze Age Jarlshofians. This layout, with the pottery type, enables us to identify these polished-stone-using farmers.

The first farmers to enter the British Isles came from the Mediterranean region. These small, brunette, peaceable and industrious people are now called Iberians (Iberia being the Roman name for Spain) though they were not necessarily from present-day Spain. They brought the house type and farm plot with them when they settled among the surviving British hunter-gatherers with whom they did not compete and therefore did not fight.

It was among these unwarlike Iberians that the Megalith missionaries spread their religion. Exactly what this was cannot ever be known, but it required the creation of great stone (megalith) structures or "temples," like Stonehenge, and religious underground tombs. Since the Megalith missionaries came from the Mediterranean region, their ideas were probably related to the Egyptians, with their great pyramidal tombs and notions of the afterlife.

While it is as missionaries that the Megalithians made their mark in prehistory, they must also have made their living in some manner. It has been suggested that they were factors, operators of trading posts, such as the Hudson's Bay Company maintained amongst the Indians. And, as with the Hudson's Bay Company, furs were probably the articles most wanted. The Ibero-British farmers, it is now thought, constructed the circular ditch and bank at Stonehenge, but it was certainly under the influence of the Megalith missionaries that the first great standing stones were set up.

At Jarlshof it seems there was never enough of a population to undertake the construction of one of the great stone communal mound tombs that marked the presence of the Megalithians as certainly as cross-topped churches now mark the presence of Christianity. Or there may be another explanation: the Jarlshofians boated their dead to one of the great communal Megalith tombs in the Orkneys, or even in Scandinavia. But if one final explanation is permissible it would be that the Jarlshofians were not that energetic in the practice of Megalithianism as such.

Perhaps they were a sect, like the Pilgrims when they sought freedom in America. Or even heretics.

The tendency might be to think of these first Jarlshofians as extremely primitive people because they were of the Stone Age. By modern standards they were, but not by contrast with the pioneers who first settled Kentucky, Tennessee and Ohio. The iron implements that were the advantage the frontiersmen had over the Jarlshofians would have been of no special benefit in the Shetlands. Iron axes were not needed because there were no trees. The long rifle was not needed because there were no human or animal enemies. The iron plowshare was not needed because the sand-mixed soil was light, and grain crops do not require deep cultivation like corn; indeed, they do not require plowing at all and can be sown with the merest scratching of the surface. Yet within a generation the Kentucky and Tennessee pioneers, despite constant Indian harassment, had made more progress, because they were in contact with a literate civilization, than was made by the Neolithic Jarlshofians during their several hundred years' stay beneath Sumburgh Head. When the sands came they found these farmers where they had been in the beginning.

There is nothing unique about Jarlshof's victimization by sea sand. Excavation in 1950–54 by R.L.S. Bruce-Mitford of the Dark Age village of Mawgan Porth on the coast of Cornwall uncovered a sizeable hamlet that was duned to death in the year 1100, approximately. The inhabitants, however, had seen the disaster coming and had picked up their belongings and walked away, setting up in a nearby spot which exists as a village today.

Much nearer the Jarlshof Neolithic people in time and geography was the village of Skara Brae, excavated by the noted prehistorian V. Gordon Childe. It was not only covered by storms, it was uncovered by one. Its people, too, had walked away with their goods and chattels, leaving behind one of the strangest habitations of man ever uncovered. Skara Brae is located on the Bay of Skail on the main Orkney Island, facing the widest reaches of the North Atlantic. The cold had come off the sea upon the inhabitants, Neolithic cattlemen who had first settled there about 3800 years ago (about the time Jarlshof was first settled), long before the sand became a menace. To shut out the cold they had deliberately buried their homes, about 8 feet in height, in their own refuse. But this does not necessarily mean that the folk of Skara Brae were unsanitary by habit. Each house had its cabinets and bureaus, made entirely of the stone of that treeless place. And one house had a privy with a drain to the outside, placed in a closet for privacy.

The archaeology of Jarlshof is now complete. Sterile sand, under which there are no further villages, has been reached with the Neolithic. This humble place has yielded no treasures to compare with the least statuette from the tombs of the Pharaohs or the smallest golden bauble from Troy. Something entirely different has come out of this record of men caught in the ebb and flow of climate. Here is an outline of, an index to, modern western and northern European prehistory.

How can any part of prehistory be called "modern"? Because this is that part of prehistory that holds the roots of the modern world. Though they used stone tools and wore leather clothing cut out with quartz knives and sewn with bone needles and sinew, these Neolithic people were modern. They were husbandmen, cultivators of food plants and managers of stock. They knew and practiced the only method of food production by which a modern population could be supported. In some places, at Jarmo in Iraq, for instance, husbandry goes back about 8,000 years. That is the reason why civilization in that region is 4000 years older than in the Western world. When hunting, fishing and the gathering of wild plants were replaced, for climatic reasons, by the herding of beasts formerly hunted; when seeds formerly gathered at random were sown; and when brittle stone that could only be chipped or rubbed into shape was replaced by metals of great tensile strength that could be cast—then the modern world was founded. As we see it now, from that point on nothing could stand in the way of civilization, not even the tyranny of climate which is certainly mankind's greatest, if severest, teacher.

Jarlshof is not important as the place where the new advances in technologies of tool making and food production took place but as an outline, an index to, these changes, by which the modern world came into being. Nothing happened at Jarlshof; it is only the result of what happened elsewhere. Its significance is that it confirms what archaeologists had already discovered had happened elsewhere. But because its changes are simple, sand-separated, and in orderly succession, we understand them better. This simplicity is not only of the succession of technologies, but of climate. Since Jarlshof is on the borderline of warm and cold climatic zones the ebb and flow of climate is here as marked as the rings on a tree.

One or two final words must be said about climatic fluctuation. Climate is always an average or a trend. During cold cycles there will be above-average years, and perhaps two or three together. Similarly, among the good weather years bad ones will be mixed in. Because human beings have intelligence and adaptability and investments in work and property, the good years during the bad periods will encourage them to hang on; and the bad years during the good periods will be endured, for mankind can and often has lived on hope. Neither the Fairbridge chart nor any other like it can be transposed into a record of human behavior. Men do not, like water, turn into ice at one precise temperature and into steam at another. All living things, and human beings most of all, can make adjustments within limits to a hostile environment.

Jarlshof, then, is a sort of reduction of "modern" prehistory to its elements. By the year 2000, or perhaps 2500, the world will have become too populated for comfort. The solution may well be new frontiers on other worlds within the solar system, or beyond. It may be reclamation of the Arctic or, if a bad turn of climate prevents that, an adjustment to living and food production in places not now considered habitable—the equatorial jungles, the great deserts, even the sea. Whatever the solution we, as archaeologists, have seen at Jarlshof elements of the problem in formation. The treasure archaeology digs for is an understanding of the present —and the future.

7

Amerind Heaps and Mounds in America

O NE OF THE MOST MISUSED and therefore misunderstood terms in American prehistory is the
name "Mound Builders."

The name as used by archaeologists designates a
people more often called by them the Hopewell people,
after the place in Ohio where one of their mounds was
scientifically dug and its contents recognized as being
of a distinctive culture. But the Hopewellian Mound
Builders did not by any means build all the thousands
of mounds that dot the landscape of the United States,
nor were all these mounds built for the same purpose.

Courtesy of Mound State Monument, Moundville, Alabama

This 20-foot-deep mound of shell and flood deposit is on the Tennessee River, 12 miles west of Muscle Shoals, Alabama, in Pickwick Basin.

Some mounds are simply middens, that is, heaps of refuse, usually shell. In the Pickwick Basin of Alabama some of these shell heaps were 35 feet high, built up by alternate layers of shell and river deposits. Amerinds lived on these shell heaps, building houses or shelters on them and burying their dead within them.

While these were man-made, they were not purposively made. They only accumulated and some would not be, perhaps, thought of as mounds by neighbors who often do not even know of their existence. This could

86

hardly be said of Green Mound, a 30-foot-high shell heap near Daytona Beach, Florida, or of Turtle Mound, about 40 feet high, just south of New Smyrna Beach. These two mounds are the most prominent features, the only "hills," on the landscape for miles along the flat seacoast. A palmetto tree growing out of the top of Green Mound was said in 1871 to have been a landmark both on land and sea, and the mound itself is referred to as early as 1696. Excavation by the archaeologist Ripley Bullen has shown that it was accumulated between about AD. 800 and 1300. This was during the same period of warm weather that covered the Viking occupation at Jarlshof.

Shellfish are very sensitive indicators of climatic change by reason of the rise and fall of the temperature of their environment, whether it be fresh water or shallow coastal sea water. The writer of this book has been engaged for several years in digging out shell mounds along the banks of the Hudson River, near Croton-on-Hudson. Though this location is about 35 miles upriver from New York Bay, the range of tide today is about 4 feet and the water is saline, making for good oyster habitat. Oysters do not grow there now, but they have been harvested within historic times. The Dutch, in the middle of the 17th century, did not consider them worth eating, but 70 years ago they were preferred by some gourmets to Chesapeake Bay oysters.

Perhaps the reason they were preferred was that they were undersized and tender. Nothing is so impressive in our excavation of these Croton oyster shell heaps as the graduation in size through climatic periods. The oyster shells cast aside by Amerinds during the very warm period either 6000 years ago or 3800 years ago reach an occasional length of 8 inches. And an 8-inch-long oyster shell is much more than double the bulk of a 4-inch-long one by reason of the accretion of plates. Intermixed with these giant (for these parts) shells are the delicate, fluted shells of the ribbed mussel. Though the ribbed mussel has always grown and still grows in the waters about Long Island, New York, it never appears again in the Croton area after the giant oyster period. Subsequent to this, oyster shell decreases progressively in size until the top deposits, dated by their pottery at about 2600 years ago (during a climatic period much like today's) are of shell the biggest of which is about 3 inches long.

Shell midden mounds are a study in themselves. There are very few water courses or bodies of water of any size in America (and very few stretches of coast) along which they cannot be found, from Florida to Maine, and from Maine to California. Along the coasts they consist of clams and oysters, certain salt-water mussels, coquina and abalone. In fresh-water streams and ponds they will consist of fresh-water mussels almost exclusively. But since these mounds are, strictly speaking, ancient garbage dumps, they will contain, in addition to castoff tools and broken pottery, fish and animal bones. Certain alkalis or carbonates derived from shell are known to be good preservatives of bone. They are, therefore, valuable archaeological sites and must be excavated just as carefully as any other type of mound or site.

Still, monuments to the presence of Amerinds that they are, middens were not deliberately constructed. No tally has ever been taken of the purposive mounds and earthworks within the limits of the United States, and if such a tally is ever attempted it can only fall short by a considerable percentage of the number that once existed. Plowing, building and looting have erased them by the hundreds, if not by the thousands. A notion of what the decimation has been can be gained from figures on some mound groups in Iowa, reported by the archaeologist Paul L. Beaubein.

The Sny-McGill concentration of mounds is located near McGregor, Iowa, where Sny-McGill Creek enters the Mississippi. Forty mounds of this group are still undisturbed, but it originally consisted of 96 mounds—85 conical mounds, 6 linear mounds, and 5 effigy mounds, two of the latter bird-shaped and three bear-shaped. Only ten miles north of Sny-McGill is an area of about 1200 acres now dedicated as the Effigy Mounds National Monument, or park. Still in existence are 62 mounds— 45 conicals, 10 linears, 4 effigies and 3 joined conicals; at least 55 others have disappeared. Of another group of 57 in the Yellow River which runs through Effigy Mound National Monument—37 conicals, 12 linear, 6 club-shaped and 3 bear effigies—only 6 conicals and 2 linears remain. Frequently enough, when the mounds

themselves still exist they have been looted by relic hunters, either private collectors or commercial merchants of
artifacts. Thus has our archaeological heritage been
slipping away from us.

All the mounds in the groups just detailed are probably
burial mounds, as are the overwhelming majority of the
labor-raised mounds in America. The most puzzling of
these are the effigy mounds, which cluster most thickly
in Wisconsin, Minnesota, Iowa and Illinois. Human
skeletal bits and pieces are usually found within them,
but without any "grave goods" to accompany the dead,
and without the signs of formal burial. Their significance
must somehow consist of their shape, usually of an animal like the bird (thought to be the thunderbird) the
bear, the turtle, and in at least the instance of the Great
Serpent Mound (with an egg in its mouth) of Adams
County, Ohio, the snake. Some of these effigy mounds
contain stone arrangements that may be crude altars,
for no recognizable rite.

It may be that they are totems, that is, clan symbols,
in which a human bone or two is included for symbolic
reasons, as we place documents and tokens in the corner-
stones of buildings. Archaeologist Beaubein explored
one of the bird effigies—more than 60 are reported in
Iowa alone—of the Sny-McGill group. It measured 158
feet from wing tip to wing tip, 78½ feet from head to
tail, and had been reduced by erosion and cultivation
to a height of 2 feet. All he found were portions of 12
teeth of a 9-year-old child and the metatarsus (a bone

in the foot) of an adult. A bear effigy from another group bore nothing at all.

True, some of these Iowan mounds, the conical ones, were either built by Hopewellians, or by a people influenced by Hopewellians, who were highly energetic raisers of burial mounds for religious reasons. But this is not the kind of mound that gave Hopewellians the right to be known as The Mound Builders. These distinguishing constructions are more properly described as earthworks, since they consisted of earthen banks or walls arranged in geometric designs—circles, rectangles, octagons and more complex figures, often lying near each other and connected by walled passageways. The banks, 12 to 15 feet high, enclose areas from 10 to 100 acres and, since they are interrupted by wide openings, are considered not to be fortifications but places of religious ceremony or "sacred precincts."

The Hopewellians did build walls of stone or earth skirting hilltop locations that must have been meant as forts, yet these too were used as sacred precincts. Burial mounds are found within them, as they are within the geometric enclosures. And there is evidence that some circular enclosures were village sites, with raised platforms in the center from which news announcements were made. All in all, the Hopewellians broke an enormous amount of ground with their stone spuds and spades, and moved it, by main strength only, in withe baskets (the imprint of dirt-carrying baskets has been found in mound fill) quite enough to give them a reputation. It has even been suggested that they overdid it, and that their decline as a culturally prominent people was due to too much earth-moving. But the archaeologist who suggested this, James B. Griffin, put it rather more nicely. He called it "cultural fatigue."

Earth-mound building among the Amerinds north of Mexico by no means died out with the Hopewellians, who seem to have begun to wane about the year 200, though their influence was felt for centuries. Some 600 to 700 years later there began to be built in the Missis-

The central tomb of a Hopewellian burial mound in Illinois, before detailed excavation.

sippi Valley the so-called temple mounds. They are flat-topped, rectangular-based pyramids in shape, with a ramp or sometimes steps leading to the top. On this platform wooden temples and other principal public buildings were erected, periodically burned—every 7 years, it is thought—and rebuilt, at which time the mound was added to. In essential form and function these temple mounds resemble the very much more elaborate ziggurats of the Sumerians, found in ancient Babylon and Assyria, though they are thousands of years

Completely excavated, the tomb reveals seven burials. A cache of fine Hopewellian projectile points was found with the upper left burial.

Courtesy of the Illinois State Mueum.

and thousands of miles apart. But the idea that caused them to be raised—the elevation of the place of ceremony to be nearer the god worshipped—appears to be very similar. As why should they not be, if each worshipped a single god, rather than a whole pantheon of gods? That god was the high god, the Sun.

The temple mound idea undoubtedly came most immediately from Aztecan Mexico, whence it had come from the Mayas of Central America. No conquering nation brought it. Indeed there is no record in the prehistory of the United States of the conquering movement of whole peoples like the Battle-Axers of 4000 years ago or the Huns of 2700 years ago. The Maya, Inca and Aztec nations all had their imperialistic eras, but north of the Rio Grande only the Iroquois, well after Columbus' day, went adventuring abroad. And they conquered tribes, not territory, and came home again to their own Long Houses after victory.

Temple mounds are indicative not of a single building plan but of an entire religious, and probably social, system. And new systems are spread by those specifically interested in spreading them. That is, priestly missionaries, like the Megalith missionaries.

We have only to close our eyes for a moment and imagine, first, a 30- or 40-foot-high square or rectangular mound with a wooden temple on top and, second, a circular embankment 6 or 8 feet high enclosing an area that may be either flat meadow or a grove of trees. Instantly it is clear how great must be the difference between the religion of the temple-mound builders of A.D. 800 to A.D. 1500 and the Hopewellian Mound Builders of 200 B.C. to A.D. 200.

At the foot of the temple mound is a plaza where the faithful congregate to observe and take part—probably a passive part—in the ritual being conducted by the priests on the mound's platform top. But it is not necessary to be in the plaza group. What the priests are doing —very likely the sacrifice of a human victim, if this religion is like that of the Aztec—can be seen from anywhere in the countryside around.

The principal ceremonial days will be Midsummer's Day, June 22, the longest day of the year, and the first day of Winter, December 21, the shortest day. The equinoxes, that is, the two days of the year when day and night are of equal length (about March 21 and September 22) will also be celebrated. Wherever there is sun worship, be it among the Aztecs or the Battle-Axers, this is the order of feasts, because the cycle of the sun is the same everywhere in the northern hemisphere. On December 21 when the sun has sunk to its lowest ebb there must be ceremonies and sacrifices to bring it back for the new year. When it is at its fullest, there must be ceremonies and sacrifices to its all powerful divinity.

The Hopewellian arrangements for ceremony could hardly be more different. The embankments are, plainly, a boundary and a wall of exclusion. The elect are allowed into the sacred precincts; others are not meant to enter. Walls always mean insiders and outsiders. Much of the ritual must be secret, and probably magical. Nothing about the location shows any special arrangement to bring light into the ritual. We are perfectly free to assume that it was more likely to have taken place under the moon than the sun. To be sure, nobody has ever seen a Hopewell ceremony or anything that could be in any way related to it. But this is not to say that the element of the occult in Hopewell ceremony is wishful thinking. There was reported in 1956 the discovery, in a Hopewell grave from Ross County, Ohio, of a mask consisting of human skull bones that had probably been sewn to a leather hood or full head mask, such as night riders are usually shown wearing. This mask is unique of its kind and construction. But it is not unique among the Hopewells as an article of priestly or shamanistic dress for the purpose of disguise or changing the ceremonial personality of the wearer.

This contrast of Hopewell and Temple Mound builder religions should not be thought of as suggesting the moral superiority of the one over the other. Both the Mayas and the Aztecs, we know, practiced human sacrifice, the Aztecs engaging in the most blood-drenched rites of any people on the American continents. When an Aztec priest ripped the heart out of a sacrificial victim with his stone knife the best vantage point from which to show it to the most people was from the height of a platform-type mound.

Whether the Hopewell religion demanded human sacrifice at all is not known to archaeology. Its use of human bones, as in the head mask, and in the manufacture of whistle-flutes, as musical instruments, may have been intended as a reverence for and a feeling of kinship with the dead, rather than callousness toward the bodies of the deceased. The Hopewellians resemble the tomb-building Egyptians in that the main concern of their lives seems to have been about the manner of their burials. The accumulation of property during a man's lifetime went toward the enriching of his grave, not his posterity. This had, probably, two purposes: to establish what had been his position and prestige in life, and to enable him to enter the next life with the honors and prestige he had gained in this.

The Hopewellians were not alone in ceremonial burial, nor were they the first Amerinds to practice it. The richest burials were those of the temple-mound builders who placed graves in their temple mounds as well as in mound tombs. But mound graves were being built as late as what are called contact times, that is, the period of contact between Indians and white man. In Wisconsin, where one such late group of mounds exists, this was quite late. Archaeologist Leland Cooper reports that he excavated one of a group of 51 mounds near Rice Lake, in Barron County, and among the articles buried with the deceased were vermilion, a lead button, and spring tweezers. Apparently these Indians, thought to have been Sioux, had quickly abandoned the use of such crude tools as mussel shells for plucking out unwanted hair (which was an Indian habit) and quickly took up the little implement which is nowadays available at ten-cent stores at the cosmetics counters.

As early as 3500 years ago there was a cult all across the northern United States and southern Canada, from Maine to Minnesota, of burial with red ochre, a powder pigment. The deceased, sometimes in the flesh, some-times as a reburied skeleton, is covered with this pig-ment. Red-ochre burials are as old as Neanderthal Man of 40,000 to 70,000 years ago. They took place in the very caves where Neanderthal Man lived and, often, under the very hearths where he cooked his food. This pattern of burial—the placing of the grave in a warm place, the burial of food as well as personal possessions with it, and the sprinkling of the body with red, the color of flowing blood and therefore of life—has been interpreted as a kind of magic to restore the dead to life. The futility of this must eventually have become apparent, and after awhile the practice could have been continued only under the impression that the dead was being readied for life in another world, from which he could not be coaxed back because it was so much happier than this one.

Red-ochre burials have appeared almost everywhere in the world at one time or another. That the prac-tice should have appeared among the Amerinds is not strange, but how it began here has no sure explanation. It is assumed that the idea came from Asia. But, as with so many other traits and habits that are assumed to have come out of Asia, the path by which it came is vague, to say the least. Which brings us, rather abruptly, to the last class of Amerind mounds, the Glacial Kames.

Among the American red-ochre burials are some which are found in natural mounds called kames. These are deposits of gravel left by melt streams along the front of a retreating glacier. Sometimes the deposits are in ridges or terraces, sometimes in mounds. Though these are not man-made, those that contain burials can be said to qualify as "Indian" mounds. The archaeologist William A. Ritchie has suggested that man-made burial mounds began to be made in imitation of these utilized kames.

The time element, at least, favors this suggestion. The Glacial Kame people of Ohio seem to have passed on ceremonial burial practices to the Adena people (like the Hopewellians, named for a Ross County, Ohio, farm where an Adena mound was excavated). They passed them on or over to the Hopewellians, who spread the practice so widely over the eastern half of the United States that it never completely ceased until almost the time when the Indian no longer dominated the country.

No better understood is the origin of the Hopewellian habit of building geometric earthworks. If it came from Asia nobody has been able to point to the place in Asia from which it came. On the other hand the Hopewellians appear in the Adena country, where the Adenans, if we have our dates right, were already building mounds of rock and dirt but no geometric earthworks except simple circles. The most curious aspect of the problem is that the largest earthwork construction—so large that it literally could not be seen until an aerial photograph disclosed it in 1953—is probably the oldest. It has been called by archaeologist James A. Ford of the American Museum of Natural History, who excavated there, the largest and most complex geometrical earthwork in North America. Located at Poverty Point, Louisiana, it is at least 2700 years old. The oldest Hopewellian earthworks are probably not more than 2500 years old. But to say that the Hopewellians learned earthwork building from the master builders of Poverty Point—and whatever religious and other cultural practices went with it—leads to the question: Where did the Poverty Pointers learn it? If Asia does not yet supply the answer, neither does Meso-America (that appendage of North America that lies between the United States and South America and includes Mexico and Central America) whence came the temple mound idea and the American sun worshippers. There is an alternative. Perhaps, for some reason we don't yet find in the excavated evidence or suspect from our general knowledge of prehistory, the Poverty Pointers invented earthworks, to enable them to live a certain kind of life in a certain kind of environment.

In the first chapter of this book it was said that there is no discovery of new fact that does not immediately flush out a whole covey of fresh questions. The belated aerial discovery of Poverty Point is a most instructive example of this observation. How is it that the earliest, or one of the earliest, examples of earthworks is the largest and most complex? Should not the earliest example be the most rudimentary, and the simplest? Archaeologically it cannot be said for certain that an earlier, more rudimentary example does not exist somewhere. The evidence is merely negative—as of now.

Mounds are not the whole of American archaeology even outside the areas of the Aztecan-Mexican, Mayan or Incan civilizations. Thousands of years of American prehistory, only some of which will be covered herein, preceded the Red Ochre people, and over perhaps two-thirds of the continent there never were any mound builders. But for the area that is now the United States the temple mound builders and the Hopewellians, with their probable relatives of Poverty Point, were the most accomplished and accomplishing people on the landscape between the years 700 and 1400. They bring Amerind culture up to, as a rough equivalent, the stage of the Neolithic farmers who spread over western and northern Europe 4000 years ago. They are, at least to our American eyes, the more colorful, being rather more barbaric and exotic than, say, the Jarlshofians, whose tools and living ways would have been familiar to our grandfathers, or at the very most, our great-grandfathers.

As at Jarlshof we shall examine these Amerind mound builders in archaeological order, from most to least recent, beginning with the scientific tragedy of the great mound of Spiro.

8

A Scientific Tragedy:
The Great Mound of Spiro

O F THE SPIRO MOUND, in Oklahoma, the archaeologist Carl H. Chapman wrote, "It was obvious
that the mound and its contents were one of the most
remarkable archaeological discoveries that had ever been
made in North America."

And the archaeologist James B. Griffin wrote, "It contained one of the most concentrated deposits of ceremonial material ever uncovered in the United States."

Neither of these two archaeologists excavated Spiro.
No archaeologists did. It was mined. Literally. By men
who tunneled into it wearing miners' lamps, brought out

their finds, including bodies of the dead, in wheelbarrows, and called themselves the Pocola Mining Company.

The Pocola venture into artifact mining for profit was one of those employment makeshifts which, like selling apples on street corners, men sometimes did in desperation during the Great Depression of the 1930s. It is only on these grounds that it can be forgiven. What it cost American archaeology is beyond estimate. The prehistory of the United States does not produce rich sites.

As has been noted before, mounds usually occur in groups. The Spiro Mound, called after a small nearby town and specifically identified as the Craig Mound, was the larger of a group of four that had probably once been separated but had washed together so that the whole thing looked like a gigantic tadpole with a fat tail. Within a radius of about a quarter of a mile there are several other mounds, including an important one called the Brown Mound. Here, then, was a center of development of one of the two most impressive prehistoric periods (the other is Hopewell) north of the Mexican border. Yet the very treasure vault of its riches, the Spiro-Craig Mound, was dug out like a potato patch and the treasures, carried away in wheelbarrows, were sold by the side of the road, as though they were farm produce in season. So much came out of Spiro Mound that the market for "Indian relics" was flooded and the prices went down to dime-store level. The Pocola Mining Company did not turn a very neat profit.

Nobody ever really saw the inside of the Spiro-Craig Mound intact, not even the members of the Pocola Mining Company. They entered the circular center room through a tunnel and saw only what could be seen with their miners' lamps. Years later they agreed, in recollection, that there were four altars placed at the cardinal points of the compass in the main room. Each had a blanket covering (of rabbit fur, feathers and vegetal fiber) and about 100 pounds of shell beads. The floor was of two layers of cedar poles, one layer lying crosswise of the other, and there may have been partial walls of cedar poles. A circular bank of shell had been laid about the tomb chamber. The diggers said that the shell had slumped and decayed and when it was removed they could walk through the tunnel thus created inside the main mound. If their observations could be believed there were but two burials in the tomb chamber, though there were perhaps twenty in the tail of three mounds attached to the principal one.

The result of the mining and the subsequent retailing of Spiro material was that priceless artifacts were scattered all over the country (some are said to have gone to France), ending up in museums and the hands of private collectors, often mislabeled, usually misunderstood.

The only hope of acquiring an archaeological knowledge of what had been in the Spiro Mound was the forlorn one of tracking down each artifact as though it were the long-lost heir to an English barony. This private detective work was, nevertheless, undertaken by Mr. and

Mrs. Henry W. Hamilton and T. M. Hamilton of Marshall, Missouri. They were surprisingly successful, either in recovering Spiro material or photographing it for record. What is now known of it is owed largely to the Hamiltons, whose re-assembly of the material has been submitted for study to a leading authority, the archaeologist James B. Griffin. Under Griffin's expert eye, which authenticated most of what the Hamiltons had brought together, some pieces turned out to be truly Indian, but not from Spiro, while a few others are undoubtedly fakes altogether; even archaeology attracts sharp operators. But this illustrates what would have happened to the Spiro treasure had the Hamiltons not gone after it when they did.

The Hamiltons were able to trace or estimate as having been taken out of the Spiro-Craig Mound the following: 123 stone or pottery pipes, 42 carved cedar masks, 11 stone or cedar effigies, 15 stone maces or batons, 19 spuds, 20 celts, 30 copper axes, 4 monolithic axes, 18 carved plummets, 500 pounds of galena balls, 5000 arrow heads, 16 polished discoidal stones, 20 polished bolt stones, 6 polished bannerstones, 1000 pounds of unworked galena, 150 copper needles, 70 pieces of embossed sheet copper, 18 "copper-covered baskets," 400 earspools of stone, 500 shell pendants, 27 engraved shell pendants and gorgets, 193 other engravings on shell, 1 quart of copper beads, 1 quart of cedar wood beads, 1 gallon of stone beads, 1200 pounds of shell beads, and 2 gallons of pearl beads.

Until another Spiro Mound is dug into, scientifically, the Spiro-Craig "Great Temple Mound" will have to serve as the prime example of what Amerinds could produce during the period of the temple mound builders. Though called the Great Temple Mound, the Craig Mound of the Spiro group is, or was, a conical burial mound. (*The Great Temple Mound*, if one mound in the country is to be so called, would be the one at Cahokia, Illinois, with three and perhaps five stepped platforms, and 1100 feet by 600 feet at the base.) Archaeologists have assigned the most spectacular Spiro material to the culmination of the Mississippi period because of the abundant presence of objects of what is now known as the Southern Cult.

A great deal more would be known about the enigmatic Southern Cult had Spiro been scientifically analyzed instead of demolished. For it must now be reported that the members of the Pocola Mining Company, having conducted their operations in strict secrecy, dissolved their partnership with a bang when the lease to dig in the mound expired, setting off a charge of black powder in the central tomb chamber. Later the University of Oklahoma moved in with an excavating team but this Humpty-Dumpty could not be put together again.

It will be unexpected indeed if any archaeological site richer than Spiro or representative of a richer culture is ever found on this hemisphere. The Southern Cult phase at Spiro dated at about A.D. 1300 was probably the height of artistic-religious activity of North American Amerinds as we now know them. We can be pretty sure that never, north of Mexico, will we ever encounter any of the kind of treasure of precious metal found at Sutton Hoo, or of precious stones as found in the Near East. Any thought of digging for archaeological treasure, if the emphasis is on the treasure rather than the archaeology, can be abandoned. The example of the Pocola Mining Company should be enough.

True, the Pocola Mining Company found two gallons of pearls. But pearls are the one "gem" of organic origin, the one precious "stone," that fades with time. Besides which, the pearls at Spiro were from river mussels, not from pearl oysters, and were not much to begin with. If you opened enough river mussels today you could probably get yourself a pearl necklace with less labor than digging out another Spiro.

9

The Southern Cult

THE PRESENCE of the Southern Cult is recognized
by the occurrence of certain art designs or motifs,
among which are the "eye-in-hand," "weeping eye" or
"forked eye," serpents (usually rattlesnakes), sun-circles,
death symbols and swastikas and Greek crosses. These
may be engraved in shells—and well over a hundred
engraved shells were in the Spiro-Craig material—
scratched or embossed in copper, engraved on gourds or
wood, or incised in pottery. This should not be taken
to mean that the Southern Cult was a mere art style or
school. But to try to say exactly what it was is only to
say less or more than the known truth.

It would be romantic to be able to say or even surmise that the Southern Cult was a secret organization among Amerinds, that the fantastic designs like the eye-in-hand were cabalistic symbols, that its high-priests or headmen ruled by terror in the night and that it was a tyranny of the occult. But Cult implements such as the ceremonial

SOUTHERN CULT MOTIFS

At upper left is a "weeping eye" design incised in a shell perforated to be worn as a gorget or breast ornament. At upper right is an "eye in hand" design. At lower left is an eagle warrior, at lower right a figure with a "speech symbol" issuing from his mouth. These were found at Spiro Mound.

spud (an implement like a hoe with straight blade instead of one at right angle to the handle, and used for ground breaking) and the monolithic ax (with both blade and handle carved from the same stone) as well as the bizarre designs and figures of jaguars and five-headed rattlesnakes, may just as easily be understood as evidence of earnest and peaceful fertility rituals.

Southern Cult objects have been found from Florida to North Dakota and as far northwest as the Canadian provinces of Manitoba and Saskatchewan. The Cult is called Southern because its objects and designs appear earliest and most profusely in the great ceremonial centers of Etowah in Georgia, Moundville in Alabama, and at Spiro.

What are we dealing with, then? Though all the advanced civilizations of America were imperialistic in some degree—the Aztecs and the Incas decidedly so—no archaeologist has found any evidence of, nor has any prehistorian suggested, a Southern Cult imperialism. (Imperialism here is used in the sense of a strong central government maintaining armies which are sent forth to conquer territories of other peoples, exacting tribute from the conquered and imposing on them the government of the conqueror.) No such thing as a Southern Cult Empire seems ever to have existed, despite the fact that the religion and government of the Temple Mound builders were almost surely the same thing, the high priest being also the head of government.

The Southern Cult reminds us more of the Megalith

Missionaries of Europe than of anything else. When missionaries first brought with them the temple-mound building idea (from Mexico as is now thought), the doctrines and ceremonies that these missionaries taught and performed on the eminence of the mound top must have had something about them particularly appealing to the people they preached to.

Now these Amerinds seem to have been leading at least a partially agricultural life. It was also among an agricultural people, the Neolithic farmers, that the Megalith Missionaries established themselves. They quickly convinced people who had a hard enough time making a living anyway that it was necessary to move huge boulders long distances, and to set them up with great labor in a certain fashion, in order to keep the favor of the Gods of Fertility and the Fields and, perhaps, to gain favorable passage into the afterlife.

In the pre-science days, it was the rituals of religion that were looked to as bringing the rain and sunshine on which fair crops depended. A priest or shaman who could make a people believe he could control the sun and other powers of nature, friendly and unfriendly, inevitably became the one great ruler and lawgiver in all matters. Any concern for pure morals, defined simply as good or bad conduct, was secondary to the concern to do the right thing so that drought or crop plagues were averted. Indeed, there is little doubt that any missionary of a new religion had either to be able to perform convincing new rituals and ceremonies or he would very likey have been burned at the stake as a charlatan.

When the temple mound-building, sun-worshipping missionaries came out of Mexico (or these doctrines were diffused from there) they succeeded because their rituals, their "medicine," seemed more powerful than what was in use. What was in use? It is almost impossible to say at Spiro, but it was probably something that resembled Hopewellianism. Hopewellian influence had certainly reached here, and had been strong in the Mississippi Valley, from which the temple-mound building period takes its name as the Mississippian.

Quite possibly, then, the building of temple mounds, so that the sun-worshipping priest could perform his rites nearer to and in full view of the sun, appealed more directly to a sense of logic about how the sun god should be worshipped. Designs like the forked eye and the rattlesnake may have had their half-frightening effect. Granting all this, what we are almost certainly dealing with in addition is something with which we are already familiar—the climate. The archaeologist Griffin is sure this is so.

The Hopewellian rise began at least 2500 years ago and was at its height at the time of Christ, A.D. 1. The Hopewells flourished until about the third century A.D.; by the fifth century they were through. Their centers were in the north, in Illinois and Ohio, a region that was bound to be adversely affected by a general drop in temperature. Since they were almost certainly a crop-raising culture—or how would there have been the food supply to support a population that built so many mounds and earthworks?—the Hopewells dwindled into decline. They had to turn more and more to hunting and gathering food for their subsistence; and hunting and gathering will not support as large a population as crop-raising, nor afford the same leisure for ceremonial expression. With Hopewellianism fading at the center, the outposts of its influence had to begin shifting for themselves.

But everywhere that Hopewellianism had been, traces of it lingered. The passage of centuries, and these centuries of trying climate, could only bleach it out. When the temple-mound missionaries came out of Mexico about A.D. 900 they came during a favoring stretch of weather. Their preaching that they could control the sun and bring better crops was borne out by a milding of the climate and good crops. We know now that the agency of good results was climate, not ritual. But the Amerinds couldn't have known about climatic cycles. These hadn't, so far as they were concerned, been invented yet.

All this is not to say that the Southern Cult as such arrived here with the first temple mound missionaries or their rituals. If it had, American prehistory would be much easier to figure out. It seems to be strictly a north-of-the-Rio Grande development. But there is such a "Mexican" look to Southern Cult objects that influences from Mexico must have reached periodically into Southern Cult areas while it was growing into full flower.

The archaeologists Philip Phillips, James A. Ford and James B. Griffin, who have done a great deal of work on the Mississippian period, consider it likely that after the temple-mound building priesthood arrived in the Mississippi Valley, perhaps as early as A.D. 800, population increased and a whole new social system formed about the temple mounds. They became village centers, with an emerging political organization under the control of the priesthood. Eventually villages began to war on villages and inevitably one strong village must have overcome several smaller ones and imposed its rule upon them. But for whatever reason, no strong enduring state seems to have grown out of these intervillage rivalries, let alone an empire.

Between the first arrival of the temple mound priesthood and the first sure signs of the Southern Cult, about A.D. 1100 at the earliest, a good three centuries passed in expanding population and developing political organization. Had there been anything aggressive or imperialistic about the Southern Cult, this spirit had what it needed to express itself—a way of life to impose and the manpower and political control to raise and support armies.

But nothing of the sort occurred. If anything, it would seem that the Southern Cult had the opposite effect, bringing a kind of religious oneness to the land. The lines of spread of the Southern Cult were not along any highways of war but along river valleys—that is, where corn agriculture was most intensively practiced. It went up the Missouri, which is how it got into the Dakotas where it seems to have changed character and to have become a bison hunter's ritual. And it followed the Mississippi, leaving the great centers of Cahokia (in southwestern Illinois) and Aztalan (in Wisconsin) to mark its progress rather than its conquests.

We have been at some pains to look for signs of territorial ambition in the Southern Cult by way of marking the difference between what was going on in America, north of the Rio Grande, and a period of prehistory already known to us in part in northern and western Europe. There the story is one of more or less constant aggression of one people against another, beginning with the Battle-Axers and ending, prehistorically speaking, after a succession of Celts, Romans and Germans, with the Vikings.

But north of the Rio Grande the two most highly developed cultures, the Hopewellian and the Mississippian, spread their gospel, so far as any archaeologist has been able to determine, only as ideas in religious ceremony and an associated art. This was not from mildness of temper. The Indian tribes the white man knew were warlike enough to satisfy us that they came from a long line of warriors. One tribe might punish another; might even wipe it out and claim its territory for hunting. But the result was never the authoritative political thing we call a state or nation. South of the Rio Grande the Aztecs and Mayas and the Incas were organized into the tightest political systems of which there is any record. It is doubtful that any group of North American Indians or Amerinds ever achieved any unity beyond that of a tribe of allied clans, or felt any loyalties stronger than the clan. In this they can be said to resemble the Celts as much as anybody in the world.

We can take it, then, that the Southern Cult was well named by prehistorians. It was a religion, absorbing enough and providing involvement enough to keep quite savage and warlike peoples from turning to war for something to give fullness and meaning to their lives. The richness of ceremonial gear at Spiro, Etowah, and Moundville, the artistry employed in its manufacture, and the hints of a gods-and-demons mythology in the art motifs, all strongly suggest this.

Among the recoveries from Spiro-Craig is an effigy pipe showing a ceremonially dressed priest figure bending over another figure with what looks like a knife. There can be little doubt that it is a representation of a ritual human sacrifice, quite Aztecan in method. It is confirmation of what was expected—the letting of fresh blood upon the earth being thought necessary to renew the fertility of the earth. But if the Mississippian temple mound builders did wholesale execution like the Aztecs, the charnel chambers full of the bones of victims, such as are found in Aztecan temples, do not appear at Mississippian sites. Human sacrifice, requiring the slaughter of thousands each year among the Aztecs, had not got out of hand, it would seem. And so we may take it that the Southern Cult did not honor an Aztecan-like war God. What filled their calendar must have been replete with something else.

We have a clue to this at Spiro in engraved representations on shell of what appears to be the Busk, or Green Corn Festival of later, Muskhogean-speaking, southern Indians. We know a great deal about this Busk or Posketa from direct observation by white men, since it was an historic occurrence. Held in late July or early August when the corn first came into milk, it was the time of celebration of the beginning of the New Year. The rituals, comprising both religious and social ceremonies, dances, and games (lacrosse and chungke) lasted many days. Its general emphasis, according to authorities, was on the idea of peace.

While the rites of the Busk may seem odd to us, there is nothing incomprehensible about them. As the New Year's Festival it was very much concerned with making fresh starts and new beginnings. All debts had to be settled and quarrels and disputes made up. Houses were cleaned, old clothing burned and replaced with new, and old tools and implements were thrown away. Both person and possessions were purified, the person by a spell in the sweat house (followed by scratching, usually with the touched jaw of the gar fish) and by downing a quart or so of the Black Drink. The Latin name of the herb from which this tea was brewed, Ilex Vomitoria, describes what it was—an emetic. It was supposed to rid a man of his sins and faults and to make room inside him for plenty of virtue.

When all persons and places had been purified, all fires were extinguished and a new fire was made in the village square or court by the head ceremonial chief. From this all fires for the new year were lighted. We do not know all the rituals and ceremonies, dances and games included in the program of the Busk. It we could read the engraving we would probably be able to piece it together. And "read" is not too far-fetched a word; for among the Spiro engravings is a series of human heads with speech symbols issuing from their mouths. This would seem to be the first usage of the device employed by cartoonists, showing "balloon" speeches coming from the mouths of their characters. The difference, of course, is that these Spiro Amerinds had no written language.

The feasting was on the fresh corn, in the same way we moderns eat it, as corn-on-the-cob. Thereafter the corn was not touched, in order to allow it to harden for winter storage and grinding into meal. The Festival ended with lacrosse being played by two teams on a field over a quarter of a mile long. Each player carried two lacrosse sticks, with spoonlike catching-throwing ends, much smaller than the sticks we use.

The Busk Festival was the most important of the year's ceremonial periods, which began in April and continued through the summer. And the Busk was followed until late in the fall by other social and/or ceremonial occasions, such as the "raccoon dance," during which masks were worn. All this added up to "a long summer ceremonial season," as the anthropologist John R. Swanton put it.

What is so significant about this? Simply that spring-summer-fall is also the war season. And you can't make war and Busk at the same time.

There was plenty of time, between ceremonial occasions, to go off on raids, and to fight single battles, as we know only too well from our bloody border history. But people whose time and interest were so dedicated to religious-ceremonial observances could never have mustered the communal effort to raise and maintain armies in the field for campaigns that might take months or years to wage. Our North American Indians and Amerinds were mighty warriors, but they were never troops.

10

The Hopewell People

WHAT MAKES the Hopewellians so attractive to us is not so much their remarkable accomplishments as the fact that we know exactly what they looked like.

We know what implements the Southern Cult people at Spiro used, and what they wore—the women dressed in fringed skirts of dyed-bark animal-hair cloth and probably shawls of the same material, while men of rank wore mantles or capes of this cloth beautifully overlaid with feathers and "straw hats" made of split cane—but we do not know their faces. It is true that certain pipe and figure effigies show us the Mississippians in recognizable features. The hawklike, Semitic nose, everted lips and slanted chin link together in a convex, unforgettable profile. But this does not convey to us the real humanity that we feel in the famous Knight figurines that came to us from the Hopewellians.

These little clay statuettes were found in the Knight Mound in southwestern Illinois and are best known from their reproductions in wax by B. M. Frost for the Illinois State Museum. There is nothing detectably ceremonial or stylized about them. They are naturalistic, human and completely winning. Of the four best known ones, two are of a young mother with her child; one is of a woman ceremonial dancer; and the other of a haughty young warrior. One statuette is of the young mother standing, with her child piggyback; in the other she is sitting, legs under her, with the child across her thighs, nursing. The dancing woman, with her turkey-feather fans, is caught in a moment of shift of balance in a heel-and-toe step; her hair-do is as fussy as any that ever came out of a modern beauty shop. The hair of the young warrior is equally elaborate, and he stands with arrogant insolence, weapons in hand, his face whitened with ceremonial paint.

After becoming acquainted with the Hopewellians of the Knight figurines it is best to turn to the Ridgley reconstruction drawings that concentrate on the details of Hopewellian dress and personal and official adornment. These instantly make us aware of the exotic nature of Hopewell. Now its strange earthworks and burial mounds begin, in our imaginations, to become the proper setting for these Midwesterners of two thousand years ago.

A Hopewellian male, reconstructed from evidence found in the Baehr Mounds of Illinois, wears a feathered cloth headpiece with a copper plume in it. (This copper plume rather than the more expected feather is a typical Hopewell trait. The Hopewell artisan liked to imitate one kind of material in another.) He also wears a "choker" necklace of bears' teeth, a longer necklace of bone and shell beads, and a breech clout on a belt; and he carries in his hands a stone celt (tomahawk head) and a clay pipe with a human portrait bowl. Another male might be wearing a pearl-and-shell breastplate and cut wolf-jaw pendants or pendant gorgets, or bear teeth at the belt. A Hopewell official in ceremonial dress has been reconstructed as wearing silver beads and a human jaw-bone pendant, a long deerskin poncho-like garment with designs in pearl beads, and a deer antler headdress of wood, leather or copper.

Hopewellian women were equally given to wearing many-stranded necklaces of shell, bone, pearls and other materials, and such baubles as wolf jaws and hawk skulls, as well as beaded armbands and bracelets or wristlets. The three women of the Knight figurines, at a quick glance, would be taken for South Sea Island belles, in their bright batik, beaded wrap-around skirts and little else except for beaded footgear of buskin type, like ankle-length slipper socks. Of the pair worn by the dancing woman, the left buskin is red, the right is black. The colorful batik effect of Hopewellian fabric was probably produced by resist-dyeing; that is, the area not to be dyed was covered with wax, which was removed by melting only after the fabric had been immersed in dye. The colors that seem to have been achievable were black, red, white, orange and purple.

Obviously these Amerinds were, at two thousand years ago, much in advance of the Shawnees, Miamis, Illinois and Wyandots who occupied the Hopewellian territory at the time the French and later the English and Colonials first entered it. This point is made thus by the archaeologist Thorne Deuel: "Perhaps the measure of differences existing between the Hopewellians and the historic tribes of the United States might correspond roughly to that between the Roman Republic at the height of its power and the political units of southern and western Europe a thousand years later."

The archaeologist Richard G. Morgan says, "The Hopewell people, on the whole, produced the best-made tools, weapons and ornaments of any group in the eastern United States." This is conservative. They also produced the most powerful, intense, influential and definable political society on any time level north of the Rio Grande. Before the Hopewellians declined they showed every evidence of being on their way to establishing a kind of cultural Amerind United States—Hopewellian influences being known all the way from western New York to east Texas and from Florida to Iowa.

Some archaeologists still think that much that was Hopewellian derived from Asia, but they are growing fewer. Any Asiatic people who would have brought such a culture to the United States region at this time would have been round-headed, and 75% of the Hopewellians were long-headed, only 25% being round-headed. (A cranium is considered round when the width is 75% or more of the length.) The round heads, moreover, at least in Ohio, show either frontal or occipital (rear) flattening. The frontal flattening is almost certainly due to head binding, the occipital flattening probably to the use of the cradle board.

The Hopewellians, it seems, simply grew up on the land as it was 2500 years ago, absorbing it and, as often happens when men of ability get to work, making something greater out of it. Who such men were and exactly what they did we are never apt to know. We have glimpses of such men in Dekanawidah and Hiawatha (not Longfellow's Hiawatha) of the Iroquois who, according to tradition, brought about the founding of the League of Five (later Six) Nations, The Iroquois Confederacy.

Elaborate Hopewellian burials with the deceased "housed" in a crypt of logs richly furnished with thousands of pearls and beautifully made pipes, celts, and other objects, still retain signs of having been sprinkled with red ochre. This trait was present in this very region, we know, from the earlier time of the Red Ochre and Glacial Kame people.

The Adena people were building burial mounds, and rudimentary earthworks, 300 and possibly 500 years before the first dated Hopewell sites. At least, the C14 dates now indicate that the Adena culture began before Hopewell and outlasted it, without ever achieving to the same heights.

Further, a people known to archaeologists as the Old Copper Culture had been working the virgin, native copper found on the ground and in lodes around Lake Superior as early as 7000 years ago, according to C14 dates. The Old Copper people did not have to know metallurgy to make the more than 20,000 tools and ornaments found in Michigan, Minnesota, Wisconsin, Iowa, Illinois and Ontario, and attributed to them. Included were weapon heads, awls, gorges, knives, chisels, crescentic ornaments, beads, fishhooks, breastplates, axes, and spuds or adzes. These were all hammered out of the "cold" nugget, though "cold" does not necessarily mean the ore was not heated a little.

It should be mentioned also that the Old Copper people, predecessors in time of the Red Ochre people, had a habit of burying tools and other personal effects with their dead, though these were buried in cemeteries rather than mounds.

Thus only two really important Hopewellian traits need explanation. One of these is the growing of corn. At least it seems that the Hopewells grew corn because kernels have been found in two Ohio mounds. This trait could hardly have come from Asia. Nor does it seem to have come from the Adenans who had tobacco but placed their food dependence on sunflower seed. This is not a bad crop to raise, when you think of it. Little weeding or cultivation is required because the sunflower simply outgrows the weeds and a good-sized flower can produce up to a pint of seeds. Corn had somehow to get to the Hopewellians from the Southwest, where the Basketmakers of this period had it, or from Mexico where it was being grown at least 6000 years ago.

The second trait under question is pottery. The pottery of the Ohio Hopewells is most closely related to that of the Northeast, where pottery is at least 3000 and maybe 4000 years old. But the pottery of Illinois—the other center of northern Hopewell—is distinctly different, and apparently derives from the South.

This brings up perhaps the most curious matter of all. The Ohio Hopewells were *the* earthworks builders. The Illinois Hopewells built plenty of burial mounds, but practically no earthworks at all. Yet if we go down the Ohio River far enough we will find the elaborate earthworks of Poverty Point which predate Ohio Hopewell as we now know it. And Poverty Point, Louisiana, and its companion site, Jaketown, Mississippi, may well hold not only the secret of where the Hopewell earthworks idea came from, but why the idea never became popular in Illinois Hopewell.

Over the ages the Mississippi River and its branches have cut a valley down through the middle of the present United States that is now about 75 miles wide. From perhaps 6000 years ago to 2000 years ago two great rivers occupied this valley, the Mississippi flowing down the west side and the Ohio the east side, some 75 miles apart. Their place of junction varied from time to time; sometimes it was in the west central part of the present state of Mississippi, sometimes in northern Louisiana, about 350 miles south of where it is now, at Cairo, in the southwestern tip of Illinois.

Of the two rivers the Ohio must have been distinctly the greater above the point of junction. Not only was the Mississippi lessened by the fact that the Ohio did not drain into it until the last 250 miles, but all the water that now drains into it from Kentucky, Tennessee and part of Mississippi drained into the Ohio.

Poverty Point itself is located in Louisiana, just below an old junction of the Ohio and Mississippi rivers, but Jaketown is on the banks of the old course of the Ohio River. If there were any earthworks at Jaketown, which was on an island, they have since been carried away, as some of the Poverty Point earthworks were carried away, by meandering of the river channel. But there are burial mounds at Jaketown as there are at Poverty Point.

This much we do know, then: when the Poverty Point culture began to trend upstream, the stream it trended up was the Ohio. From Poverty Point to Jaketown, and from Jaketown to the Ohio Hopewellian earthworks near Cincinnati (on the Miami River), to the Hopewellian center at Portsmouth and Hopewell itself near Chillicothe (both on the Scioto River) and to the noted earthworks at Marietta on the Muskingum, it is easy canoe water all the way, without a portage. The Miami, Scioto and Muskingum are all main streams that flow through Ohio Hopewellian earthworks territory southward into the Ohio.

Griffin, the Hopewellian authority, says of Ohio Hopewell that it "marked a high peak in ceremonial and artistic forms based on a long tradition of cultural development in the area." What we may now deduce is that the earthworks building idea was brought up the Ohio and caught on among the Ohio Hopewellians at the time they were coming into their full vigor. Only a vigorous and prospering people would have responded to such a labor-making idea so diligently.

It may now be guessed that the Illinois Hopewellians did not throw themselves into earthwork building for one of two reasons: either they did not believe in it, their older traditions being such that earthworks building was foreign to them, or they did not need to build earthworks, since those in Ohio supplied the ceremonial need for such "sacred precincts" and Ohio centers became a group of ceremonial Romes to which all roads led.

The earthworks of the Ohio Hopewells, who also raised their share of burial mounds, were not made, as children make mud pies, for the fun of it. All this labor must have been inspirited by a great faith. It was a faith with enough appeal to spread over much of the heart of the present United States, so that it became almost a "national" faith among the Amerinds, if we may use the

word national here. Yet some such word must be used
because it was a creed, a system of rituals and observances and possibly a kind of social and political organization that brought Amerinds together and made them
more, rather than less, alike. It did not cause divisions
and wars, as we see it now, but promoted a peaceful
political and cultural stability. Even the Adenans, who
remain distinct and apart from the Hopewellians during
most of the period of co-existence of the two cultures,
seem to have finally taken on a Hopewellian coloration.
And through the heavy overlay of the later Mississippian
culture there can be clearly discerned the Hopewellian
base.

Was this religion sun worship? Or ancestor worship?
Or an animal cultism? Archaeology cannot yet say. The
wolf jaws and other animal skeletal parts worn by the
Hopewellians—probably not for sheer adornment but
to ward off evil or invoke protective powers—give a clue.
Masks and ceremonial garb, the sacred precincts within
the earthworks; the burial preparation for an after-life,
using red ochre and "killing" implements and possibly
persons to accompany the spirit of the deceased—all
these are visible enough clues, since we have seen their
like in other cultures throughout the world. But what do
they add up to? To something as rich, in its way, no
doubt, as the theological myth patterns of the Teutonic
tribes, with their Odin and Thor, or the Greeks and
Romans with their Zeus–Jupiter, or the Egyptians with
their complicated godhead of Atum-Horus-Osiris-Ra.

Yet we do not know what this was, and we may never be able to puzzle it out. Most scholars feel that there were elements in it, such as Michabo, the Great Hare, that have come down to us in Algonkin mythology. But if the Algonkians were either lineal or cultural descendants of the Hopewellians, the descent was steep.

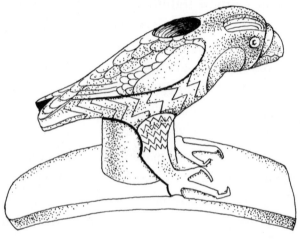

PLATFORM PIPE

This Hopewellian-type platform pipe with bird effigy bowl is probably the most famous and best known prehistoric Amerind artifact.

What do we think we know about what Hopewellian beliefs produced in cultural ways? For one thing there seems to have been a caste system. Probably at the top of the ladder were the priest-shamans, "medicine-men" with the power of final decision.

After the caste or castes of religious and secular officials would probably come that of the artisans. All authorities on Hopewell agree that the articles of fine craftsmanship, the effigy pipes, the carving, the delicate flint working and even the best pottery were the products of a relatively few hands. The designs are much too similarly and handsomely executed and the products are much too uniform all through Hopewellian territory to suggest anything but a tight guild of the highly skilled as the makers. Besides, the abundant articles of ordinary use, found on village sites, are of indifferent workmanship. Since the finely crafted articles all appear to be ceremonial or ritual in function, the craftsman's guild or caste must have been closely related to or under the supervision of the official-religious leaders.

It is strictly a guess that there was a warrior caste, though close study of the Knight figurine warrior will make it seem not a bad one.

DECORATED POTS

These, used for ceremonial occasions, are Hopewellian in design. The incising was done with a pointed stick or stone.

The actual evidence of caste stratification is from burials. These indicate only an upper class, given mound burial and rich grave goods, and a commoner class, simply interred with only an occasional article of distinct Hopewellian design. But where there are such clear divisions between the honored and the unhonored there are usually shadings of social status, based on function.

The existence of a special class of craftsmen is a near certainty, of a soldier caste conjectural, and of another which we will call traders, a possibility.

The far wanderings of Hopewellians, using the great Ohio and Mississippi river systems as their highways, certainly must have been conducted or guided or headed by men of experience who knew the "roads" they traveled and were able to communicate with the people they met. To call these men traders is hardly stretching a point, for the securing of all kinds of exotic materials for Hopewellian center craftsmen was one of the reasons, at least, for the travel. Spreading the gospel of Hopewellianism, or contact with Hopewellian congregations, may have been the prime objective, but the strange things that came home with the missionaries or traders or emissaries were astonishing.

The find of an oceanic busycon (conch) or cassis (popularly called "cameo" or "helmet") shell in an Ohio or Illinois Amerind grave will get it labelled Hopewellian at once. Beads of the marginella shell, found along Atlantic shores from the Carolinas to Florida, are common. From somewhere in the West—in the Rockies from

Alaska to Mexico—the Hopewells brought home obsidian, the volcanic rock that looks like broken glass. They particularly sought such items as grizzly bear teeth, alligator teeth, shark teeth, barracuda jaws and marine turtle shells. Where they got the meteoric iron, or the small amount of gold they worked, nobody knows. But copper and silver came from the Lake Superior lodes and galena (lead ore) from Missouri. From the Appalachian Mountains came mica and graphite, steatite (soapstone) and quartz crystals. Mussel pearls, the beautiful, multi-colored Flint Ridge (Ohio) chalcedony, and Ohio pipestone and fire clay, they already had at home. But for brown chalcedony they went all the way to Dakota, apparently because of the rich color.

What we see, then, as our eyes look backward and downward into archaeological time, and we stretch our brains piecing together the clues, is an Amerind culture seated in the heartland of the United States quite different from the sectional tribalism that the English, Dutch, French and Spanish found here at their first contact with Indians.

That this empire may have been given some political form by force of arms we cannot say for sure. We can only say there is no evidence of it; almost positively there were no Hopewellian armies, such as the Aztecs and Incas put into the field. What we, as archaeologists, discern is the substance of a way of life under which people were willing to live for well nigh a thousand years. What was it that kept them content, industrious, pacific and stimulated until the climate—and perhaps some such other adversity as epidemic disease—brought it all to a halt? Though archaeology will continue to probe for the nature of Hopewellianism, we can never know truly these remarkable people who were our ancestors on the land, though not, of course, of blood. These were the Americans who undoubtedly thought out and told the richest text of myth about the mountains, streams, the natural beauties and the seasons of the land with which we are as familiar as the ancient Greeks were with Mount Olympus and the Hellespont. As inheritors of the culture of western civilization it is right that we should know and love the myths of Greece and Rome, of the Norse-Teuton-Battle-Ax Aryans who gave us, at a minimum, the names of our days of the week, and of the Semites who gave us the Bible. It is equally right that we know the mythology that relates to the land we live in—if we can only discover what it is.

11

The First Permanent Settlement North of the Rio Grande

THE SIX concentric octagonal earthen embankments that make up the earthworks at Poverty Point, Louisiana, have been dated at about 800 B.C. by C14. Any way you look at them they are the largest Amerind structure approximating this age in the Western Hemisphere. On such a large scale is this structure or series of structures that the embankments were not known to form an integrated design until they were seen from the air in 1953.

This is understandable in view of the fact that a section of the design was washed away long ago by the flooding

American Museum of Natural History

AERIAL VIEW OF POVERTY POINT SITE

This photograph, taken by Junius Bird, shows the value of air reconnaissance in archaeology. The geometrical pattern of the ancient site was not suspected from the ground.

of the Arkansas River. Assuming the design to have consisted, in its prime, of six complete concentric octagons, the amount of earth moved to erect it came to 530,000 cubic yards. The archaeologist James A. Ford, who directed the major dig at Poverty Point, reminds us that this is 35 times the volume of the great pyramid of Gizeh.

In all, over 11 miles of banks were piled up, about 27 yards wide and from 5 to 10 feet high. More than half a million tons of earth had to be carried, in baskets each containing about 50 pounds, to heap up these earthworks.

Nor is this all there is to the Poverty Point site. Accompanying the geometric earthworks is the second largest mound in America (the mound at Cahokia is the largest.) Shaped like a flying bird, it is 70 feet high, 700 by 800 feet at the base, and adds another 185,000 cubic yards to the earth the Poverty Pointers had to dig up and carry. Since a laborer with a modern steel shovel would be hard put to dig and load two cubic yards of dirt in an eight-hour day (a cubic yard of dirt will fill the bed of a good-sized truck), it is evident that there was very little loafing at Poverty Point for many years.

About a mile away and very nearly as large as this mound is a second, which, like the first, seems to be a flying bird effigy. It is 56 feet high and 400 x 600 feet at the base.

These two mounds represent, it has been figured, about five and a half to six million man-hours of labor. In addition there exists a third mound, a conical burial mound that probably brought the total mound-building time to an even six million man hours.

Since all this earth moving had been completed at least 200 to 300 years before Hopewellianism appeared definitely on the scene; and since the Poverty Point earthworks are geometric in design, have "gateway" gaps in them and are accompanied by effigy and burial mounds, it would be very hard to avoid the conclusion that Poverty Point had a fatherly role in Hopewellian culture.

One difference must be immediately noted. Some Hopewellians lived inside their earthworks; some lived outside them. But the Poverty Pointers lived on them. It must have been quite a sight, from the nearby peak of the 70-foot high mound to look down on the bustling village of Poverty Point. The houses were arranged neatly in six octagons, the outer one of which was three-quarters of a mile in diameter, and the octagons were separated by the similarly octagonal lines of the trenches between mounds.

And surely, if the earthworks ridges were the dwelling area, the whole village, at least for a while, must have been in use. This design is, after all, basically a simple one, repeated over and over as the Poverty Point population increased steadily during the warm period in the Fairbridge scale. Plainly enough the whole design had to begin with a single octagon of earthworks that enclosed a plaza or court which was very likely for ceremonial-governmental functions. Had there not been a steady increase in population there would have been no need for the second, third, and even more octagons.

There is, however, an alternative explanation: that each successively larger octagon represents a separate later village, the earlier, smaller ridge village being abandoned when the next later, larger one was built. The Iroquois, for instance, were in the habit of abandoning their villages every ten to twelve years. But the reason for this was exhaustion of the corn lands and fuel wood in the vicinity. The Iroquois, and most other wood-land tribes which engaged in agriculture, then moved to an entirely new location.

Since the village vicinity was not changed, a succession of ridge villages at Poverty Point needs some other explanation. If this succession did occur the reason could only have been ritualistic.

We know that the temple mound builders, following Mexican rituals, periodically burned the temples and public buildings on top of their pyramidal mounds, covered the old surface with a fresh mantle of earth, and built new buildings. The motives, or inspiration, for this were both mixed and simple. As the Busk was a ceremony of purification and fresh beginnings for the new year, so this burning and rebuilding was a ritual purification and the beginning of a new era or cycle of years. This cycle may have been the 52-year span that the Aztecs observed between their New Fire ceremonies. If so, it would give Poverty Point a life of something over 300 years, which happens to correspond with the C14 dates obtained.

In interpreting the Poverty Point earthworks both possibilities must be kept in mind: (1) that it was a single village with all ridges simultaneously occupied, not only by natural increase in population but also by tribes attracted to whatever was the attraction at Poverty Point; or (2) it was a succession of villages and its design merely a repetition of a very simple earthwork embankment idea.

Archaeologists have not had much success in finding the origin of the embankment idea. Consequently some have assumed that it must have come from Asia and cite the flake "blade" making technique, a widespread technique during the Mesolithic period (before the Neolithic) as evidence of the migration. This does not seem too likely, for the "blade" making technique was being used among Alaskan and Canadian Amerinds at least 6000 years ago. A very well-developed microlithic industry of this age was discovered by J. L. Giddings at Cape Denbigh on the coast of Alaska in 1948. It is described as "microlithic" (*micro*——small, *lithic*——stone) because the flake "blades" which were struck off prepared stone cores are between an inch and two inches long. Micro-blades are found in large numbers at Poverty Point type sites. Thus micro-blades were in the Western Hemisphere at least 2000 years before any earthworks began to be built at Poverty Point.

The magnitude of the Poverty Point earthworks is what makes them seem too advanced to have been the first earthworks, and so archaeologists could only think that a people who customarily built earthworks must have migrated to Poverty Point from Asia with no stopover between. But, as has been pointed out, the Poverty Point octagons are a basically simple idea repeated six times. Is there a place where this idea is carried out only once?

In their report on the Jaketown site, archaeologist Ford and his collaborator Philip Phillips mention that single circular embankments of shell occur in several places along the Georgia coast. In one of these, on Sapelo Island, were found the baked clay balls called "Poverty Point objects" which occur so plentifully at Poverty Point, Poverty Point Plantation and Jaketown. Even more interesting is the C14 date on this Sapelo Island material. It is approximately 3800 years ago, a thousand years earlier than Poverty Point.

Immediately, of course, there comes to mind that other circle of shell, reported to have been in the Craig Mound at Spiro. Could that shell circle have been in existence when the Craig Mound was built over it? Since Craig was not excavated scientifically we will never know. The report does not sound as though it were fiction or fancy, for the miners were not archaeologists and could not have known that the presence of a circular bank of shell had any significance. This is only another example of the loss suffered at Spiro. Had any datable material been saved from that shell circle—and an archaeologist would have saved it—we might be very much better informed about the origin of Poverty Point earthworks than we now can claim to be.

The Georgia coast shell circles were lived on, like the Poverty Point embankments. They must have been smelly neighborhoods; under certain conditions shell heaps stink to high heaven. Let us, however, suppose they represent the first examples of the geometric embankment idea. What caused the Poverty Point people to adapt embankments and to elevate their houses above the general ground level? Ford tells us it was not because of the flooding of the Mississippi, which was then a mile away and is now 25 miles away. Besides, the Poverty Point site is on Macon Ridge, 15 feet above the flood plain.

For a clue to this bank top habitation we will go to the Mexican state of Chiapas where the archaeologist S. Robert Russell reported in 1954 the finding of some ruins which consisted of stone houses built on large platform mounds of gathered stone. One of these mounds or platforms was about 200 x 400 feet at the base; another was 600 x 800. The date of these ruins has been guessed at 300 B.C., which would take them out of consideration as a cultural influence on Poverty Point. What does interest us is why a primitive people went to all the trouble to pile up these stones, some of them over 10 tons in weight, just to build houses of stone on them. The answer almost certainly lies in the climate. The valley wherein these ruins lie has a "very prolonged rainy season" and is "heavily overgrown with rain forest." According to Russell, archaeological work could be carried on here only three months of the year. Which means that for nine months of the year this was a very damp location indeed.

It may now be safely surmised that the builders of these Chiapas stone mounds wanted their homes on stone where they didn't have to fight the rapidly growing vegetation constantly and where they were above the damp and the ground water. Similarly, we may surmise that the Poverty Pointers lived on embankments to be above the damp and out of reach of the effects of the ground water from the sudden, torrential thunderstorms for which the Mississippi Valley is noted.

We may never know for sure whether this is the explanation for Poverty Point's ridgetop village or whether it is something entirely different—a superstition, a religious practice, a health measure having to do, perhaps, with malaria fever, or some idea of defense. And then again the explanation may turn up, clear and unmistakable, in a single day's digging in the right place.

No such mist of uncertainty hangs over the baked clay balls that were once so puzzling they were called simply "Poverty Point objects." The reason is that Ford and Phillips found them, finally, in a place where their use became obvious. Ford estimates that the Poverty Pointers made some 20 million of these "balls"—though the sphere is only one of the many more or less standard shapes—baked as hard as brick from plain old Mississippi mud. There is only one article of usage which the Amerind would have required of this shape and hardness, and in these numbers—cooking stones. And there are no natural stones in the silted-up Mississippi Valley.

But what in the world are cooking stones? To the Amerind housewife before the days of pottery they were a matter of daily need. The Amerind could make baskets tight enough to hold water, but the water in these baskets could not be turned into soup or stew by adding meat, fish, and vegetables and then cooking the contents because the baskets could not be placed over a flame. Whereupon an unsung genius bethought herself of the idea of heating stones and throwing them in the basket "pot" until the potage was cooked to edibility. This "boiling stone" idea need not have been spontaneous. It could have been suggested by the use of beds of stones called "fire stones" laid over beds of hot coals in pits for the roasting or broiling of meat, fish and game.

The Poverty Pointers had quite evidently become familiar with these culinary techniques before they settled in the stoneless Mississippi Valley or they would have had no inclination to make imitation stones. Possibly, in the beginning, they did have to make trips to the nearest supply of stone, about 30 miles away, until the substitution of mud balls for natural stones was thought of. They had to travel that far, and ever farther, for their supplies of flint, galena, sandstone and steatite.

On the other hand, the occurrence of these baked clay balls has been noted at Sapelo Island at about 3800 years ago. This can only mean that the baked "stone" idea was distinctly east of the Mississippi 1000 years before Poverty Point and the Poverty Pointers had no need to invent it. But Sapelo Island is not the earliest C14 dated find of baked clay cooking stones. They are known from a site in California at about 4000 years ago, where baked clay objects, not all of which are cooking "stones," are as plentiful on a few sites as they are at Poverty Point and Jaketown.

One find of these Poverty Point objects that interests

us is a cache of 200 found on the Indiana side of the Ohio River just below Louisville. The cache came from a bank near a shell midden of pre-pottery people. But what would an Ohio river-bank inhabitant need clay stones for? The river bed is full of stony ones. The cache points very clearly to the probability that Poverty Point travelers came this way and brought their own cook ware. When they tired of lugging these around, there being plenty of natural stone handy, they wisely unloaded them into a hole in the ground.

Poverty Point objects show up at many Amerind sites long after ceramic cooking pots began to be made. No longer needed as "boilers," in stoneless localities they could still have been serving as "fire-stones." But their scarcity in later-than-pottery occupations suggests they are no longer utilitarian; some new use—as gaming stones, it has been suspected—apparently had been found. Thus they are not peculiar to the Poverty Point culture people, but their manufacture and usage in such prodigious numbers certainly is.

Since these objects have not been described up to now, it might be thought they are too drab to merit description. This is not so. They are not works of art; neither are they mere lumps. Ford and Phillips have separated them into four common types, with perhaps a dozen uncommon types in addition. The uncommon types do seem to represent an execution of intentional, usually symmetric, form. The common types are those showing only as much effort as was required to shape a usable stone. Except for one thing: they are cylindrical and grooved around or longitudinally. The grooves are finger marks of the hand that made and last grasped the object and left its imprint deliberately. To lay your own fingers in the same grooves is like shaking hands with an Amerind housewife dead for almost three thousand years.

One of the uses to which the profusion of Poverty Point objects can be put is in archaeological argument. Hunter-gatherer-collector Amerinds could not live in one spot very long because the game was soon thinned out and the nuts, berries or other local product soon harvested; they could not live in large, permanent villages at all. Yet the 20 million or so clay cooking balls estimated by Ford tell us that Poverty Point was a permanent village occupied continuously for hundreds of years. The conclusion is inescapable, despite the fact that archaeology has not yet been able to uncover the evidence: the Poverty Pointers raised crops—probably the Amerind trinity of corn, beans and squash—on the nearby flood plain of the Mississippi. Because it was a flood plain, it had its fertility annually renewed by the spring high water. There are no hills of midden shell at Poverty Point, as there are in Pickwick Basin, Alabama, to show that shellfish supported the population. What the clay balls tell us is that a great many generations of Poverty Pointers ate, if not well, then regularly.

Now that we have a good look at the Poverty Point culture we can make up our minds about its relation to Hopewell. Most archaeologists working in Amerind cultures have made up theirs, subject to change at any new evidence. Griffin thinks Poverty Point is a sort of grand-father to Hopewell; that is, one of three or four ances-tors. Ford has expressed himself as believing the Hope-wellians came downriver and imposed themselves on the Poverty Point area population. And there are other views, all of which have something to recommend them.

The strong resemblances between Poverty Point and Hopewell have already been enumerated: geometric earthworks, effigy mounds, burial mounds, some sort of

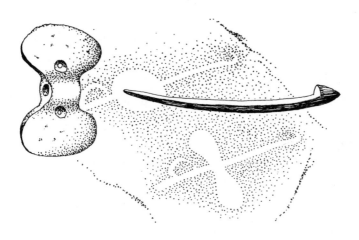

ATLATL AND BANNER STONE

In the background of these depictions of an atlatl and a banner stone is a pictograph carved in rock, by the Amerind users them-selves, of an atlatl with banner stone attached. Some banner stones, like the one shown, were bored through and slipped onto the atlatl. Others were simply tied on or, possibly, slotted into it. The banner stone was a weight that added force to the spear cast.

horticulture or agriculture to support this population of earth movers; use of the atlatl or throwing stick with attached bannerstone to weight it, polished stone axes, bird effigies, the Mesolithic "blade" making technique, the production of quantities of beads, the use of pipes, fascination with exotic materials which both were willing to go a long way to get. The Poverty Pointers brought back Great Lakes copper, Appalachian range steatite, Arkansas quartz crystals and magnetite (iron ore), and Missouri galena.

Compared with these similarities the differences appear to be no more than might have been expected between a progressive descendant and a vigorous ancestor. The Hopewells did not use clay balls—they did not have to—nor that interesting weapon, bola stone. (This is the bolas now known from use by Argentinian cowboys. It consists of three weights or stones tied together by lengths of hide thong or twine. When cast, the weights cause the thongs to wrap about the legs of the target, throwing it to the ground. The weights can also stun or kill when the target is a bird, as it often was.) Certainly Hopewell pottery did not come from Poverty Point, or even from that direction. And there is little likelihood that the two peoples spoke the same language or were of the same blood line. The conclusion must be, then, that the Hopewell people, or their leaders at least, were familiar with the Poverty Point culture, took from it what they wanted, and improved on it according to their genius. Or, again, the Poverty Pointers may have sent missionaries into the Ohio country where they spread their gospel among a people ripe for it.

The presently known C14 dates make it necessary to consider Poverty Point ancestral to Hopewell. But what is ancestral to Poverty Point nowhere appears on the landscape except as we have picked up vague references from here and there. It appears, in our current knowledge, that a great many cultural traits that were in the air at the time suddenly came to roost at Poverty Point and produced the first break away from the old hunting-gathering pattern and the first real permanent settlement north of the Rio Grande. These Poverty Pointers are, it would seem, the best candidates for our first North American Neolithic farmers. They are undoubtedly one of the most interesting unsolved problems in American archaeology.

12

Mankind's First True Village

IN ARCHAEOLOGY the statement that this thing or that thing was the first must be handled with great caution. We rarely have sufficient knowledge about any aspect of prehistory to substantiate such definite conclusions. Because archaeologists dig for the roots of institutions, technologies, living patterns, traits, and so forth, they are always finding something a little older, a little "firster." So they shy away from proclaiming precedents. But it must be admitted that when a definition has been properly stated, there must be a first thing that conforms to it or there would never have been any reason for setting up the definition in the first place.

When Poverty Point is spoken of as possibly the first permanent village north of Mexico, it should be explained what is meant.

A true village cannot exist until horticulture or agriculture begins to be practiced, because it alone provides a consistent and fixed-locale food supply. If our deductions about garden or field crops at Poverty Point are right then it is our first true village north of Mexico, being our first example of a food-raising rather than food-gathering culture.

Possibly the first clusters of habitation that had a permanent look to the casual eye would have been found on top of the Pickwick Basin shell middens in Alabama at about 7000 years ago. Turtles, fish, and shellfish—56 varieties of mussel and 22 varieties of freshwater snails large enough to eat—afforded a stable enough quantitative food supply to warrant the building of fixed structures nearby. Archaeologists William S. Webb and David I. DeJarnette, who excavated these shell middens, found the post molds in the ground—that is, the holes in the ground left by the rotted-away structural posts—but were not able to figure out the pattern. What happened was that flooding regularly wiped out these huts and when the villagers returned after the subsidence of the water they rebuilt on the same site, thus confusing the pattern of post molds. The structures were undoubtedly flimsy, as they would have been meant to be, since there was little likelihood that they would remain standing longer than a year or two. Probably they were made as

"wigwams" were made in historic times, by setting small posts in a circle or oval, bending them toward the center and lashing them together. This framework was then covered with bark or skins.

The hunter-collector band of semi-nomads was usually what is called an "extended family." All its members were in direct line of descent, except for husbands and/or wives. When a mussel-rich shoal in a fish-teeming river drew together two or three of these extended families for prolonged periods of cohabitation, a new pattern of society had to be established. This is the beginning of what village life means—the association of families, each of which has its own "natural" head man in the grandfather or his son. Then it must be determined who is or who are the leader or leaders, and customs—or laws, if you prefer—must be established to promote peaceable living together.

Courtesy Ashley Studio, Bridgewater, Mass.

Diorama of Wapanucket No. 6 Village as it can be seen in the Bronson Museum, Attleboro, Mass.

The Pickwick Basin "villages" thus had the social elements of a village, but economically they were only camps and collections of hearths, without the kind of permanence that comes from laboriously built structures and the resultant sense of property. Furthermore, these "villages" would probably have been seasonally occupied, with the whole population trooping off during certain harvest seasons for nuts, berries and edible roots. There is not enough of carbohydrate in an all-fish or all-meat diet to keep the human stomach satisfied.

A site which comes a little closer to our conception of a village as a permanent community of persons and structures, with an appropriate social organization, has been found on the shores of Assawompsett Lake, in Massachusetts. It is called Wapanucket No. 6 and has been

C14 dated at about 4250 years ago, or about 2200 B.C. Post molds outlining, presumably, at least seven round family-size dwellings of from 30 to 46 feet in diameter were discovered. An eighth structure, 66 feet in diameter, is interpreted as a ceremonial center or, what would probably be a better term, a council house. A well-established pattern of village organization is implicit in such a settlement layout. Its inhabitants were accustomed to acting together communally and to thinking of themselves as belonging to a social unit larger than the family band. (Some of the burials, incidentally, were with red ochre and "killed" artifacts.) Many Indians of the Northeast were no better organized than this at the advent of the white man.

But Wapanucket No. 6, sometimes called (and with considerable justice) the oldest known aboriginal American village, is still not fully a village. Its people were still in the hunting-gathering stage of economy and perforce had to leave the village at intervals. Maurice Robbins, who directed the excavation of Wapanucket No. 6, outlines the way of life of these Wapanuckettes as dependent on the annual spawning runs of salmon and the alewife (which were smoked for preservation), on shellfish, nuts (including acorns), berries, and game.

Is there such a thing as a first true village in the career of mankind?

There is, and at the present time the title belongs to the Qalat Jarmo site, in Iraq. We would expect to find it there, in the Near East, where nearly all the early great civilizations flowered out of the roots of the cultivation of barley and emer wheat and the domestication of food animals. Here is where both the plants and animals that were first domesticated existed in the wild state and so presented man with the opportunity he eventually seized of turning them into "crops."

The first C14 dates on Jarmo, excavated by Robert J. Braidwood in 1948, gave a date of about 6700 years ago for the founding of Jarmo. A later series of C14 dates has lengthened this to about 8700 years. It seems very unlikely that a true village, as we have been defining it, will be found at a significantly earlier time than this. The houses were made of pressed mud; about 30 of them appear to have been occupied at a time, and the population has been calculated at about 200. Jarmo must have been something of a metropolis, for instead of using the local flint for their microliths the Jarmoans imported obsidian from 400 miles away. These microliths were used, among other things, for sickle blades, being set end to end along handles of wood or bone. The polish imparted to the edges by cutting grain still shows glossily on the specimens picked up by archaeologists thousands of years later.

The Jarmoans raised two kinds of wheat, an unidentified legume (beans are legumes) and pigs, cattle, a sheeplike goat, a species of horse and the dog. We wonder whether his economic security, his pendants, beads and marble bracelets, a clan symbol impressed on him in red ochre by a pottery stamp, did not make the prosperous Jarmoan consider himself very sophisticated and advanced, by comparison with the hunting bands of the hills. The truth of the matter is that he was. Farming was not old-fashioned then, as we are inclined to think it even now when it is done with the most modern equipment. It was decidedly new-fashioned, as new as electronics is to us, and, in the long view, more important to the human race. Jarmo was the leader, or one of the leaders, of the agricultural revolution, the first of the world's two most important economic revolutions. The other is the industrial revolution.

As a village Jarmo was a success. Braidwood found 12 different levels, each identified by a difference in architecture. It shows, therefore, the permanence we have been thinking of as essential to a true village. How important this permanence is can be clearly seen from a site not far from Jarmo, called Karim Shahir. What was found here—microliths, stone hoes and grain-milling stones—gives evidence of a beginning agriculture, but without a permanent village. Braidwood considers that it was occupied only seasonally. So Karim Shahir represents agriculture without structurally permanent dwellings. Obviously these Shahirans were going no place until they settled down. Perhaps they did, a little later, go and settle down—at Jarmo.

Jarmo itself never became a great city, but out of what was begun there grew the ancient Sumerian and Akkadian kingdoms of the Tigris and Euphrates Valley, the eastern horn of which was aptly named the Fertile Crescent by the historian James H. Breasted, the western horn of which was Egypt. Jarmo is in the hills that wall in the eastern edge of the Tigris Valley; and the natural habitat of wheat is hill country, not the river valley. The Jarmoans had not only begun the agricultural revolution, they had begun the transformation of wheat from a wild mountain grass to a grain domesticated in the rich bottom lands of the Two Rivers where it could flourish as it had never flourished in its mountain meadows.

Within about 3700 years of Jarmo's beginning, history had dawned in both horns of the Fertile Crescent. Records were being written down in majestic cities that had advanced as far beyond Jarmo as we have advanced beyond them.

But when we touch history we touch what we are not prepared to deal with in this book. What has been made known by archaeology about Egypt and the succession of kingdoms of Asia Minor, and of the whole eastern end of the Mediterranean, including Greece and the Island of Crete, is more than anybody knew at any time in that ancient world. Volume after volume has been written about the Egyptians, the Minoans, the Hittites, the Babylonians, the Greeks and Trojans, and it is to these books that the reader must go for stories so complex.

As with the civilizations of the Near East, so it is with the high cultures or civilizations of America—the Mayan, the Incan and the Aztecan. These are tales told before, in books that will richly repay the reading. To know only a smattering about these peoples is not to take advantage of all that is known.

But there is one civilization of the ancient world, as advanced as the civilizations of Egypt and Mesopotamia, and approximately as old, with a form of writing we cannot yet read, which has received much less than equal publication. Most fairly well-read people could at least locate on a map the homelands of the Mayas, Incas and Aztecs, and the Minoans, Sumerians and Egyptians, but it is the rare person who has even heard of the twin cities of Harappa and Mohenjo-Daro.

13

The Best-Planned Cities
of the Ancient World

T HE KINGDOM of which Harappa and Mohenjo-Daro were the twin metropolises is called Harappa, after one of the cities, which in turn takes its name from a modern village on the site. Nobody has the slightest idea what these Harappans called themselves or their land, even though they were widely literate and both names may appear many times in the samples of their pictographic writing that have been recovered.

The kingdom of Harappa lay in the valley of the Indus River, mostly within the modern state of Pakistan. It seems to have had a seacoast of about 600 miles on the

Arabian Sea and to have extended perhaps 1000 miles inland. Mohenjo-Daro and Harappa, almost duplicates of one another, were about 400 miles apart. Mohenjo-Daro was on the Indus, Harappa on one of its main branches, the Ravi River. Each was square in plan and covered about a square mile in area. Each had a population of about 20,000—and this estimate should be quite accurate, for so neatly planned and laid out were these two cities that the inhabitants must almost have been pigeon-holed or filed. The population of the kingdom, territorially larger than Egypt and seven times larger than Sumer, was perhaps 100,000. More than 60 Harappan towns, villages and trading posts have been excavated or recorded and Stuart Piggott, who is Harappa's principal prehistorian (there have been several excavators), believes many more are awaiting archaeological attention.

Two entirely unrelated facts interest us about the Harappans, beyond the discovery that they built a major civilization independently of the civilizations of the Fertile Crescent. The kingdom, after reaching full flower about 4500 years ago, and lasting 1000 years unchanged, was levelled to the ground by our old acquaintances, the Battle-Axers.

And the Harappan achievement, among hundreds, that most interests us is their bathroom. There is something peculiarly modern about inside toilets, representing as they do a concern for sanitation that has been rare throughout history, not to speak of prehistory. The Harappan bathrooms had paved floors, with drains leading into an underground system of sewage mains complete with manholes for access in cleaning. But the manhole covers were not iron; they were of tile. When you find in the wall of an Harappan house an opening for the disposal of trash into a brick bin outside you realize that the Harappans of Harrappa and Mohenjo-Daro must have had the neatest, cleanest, best planned, best organized city of the ancient world and one that would put most modern cities to shame.

The material of Harappan civilization was brick, very modern looking in that it is standard-sized (11″ x 5.5″ x 2.5″), is baked instead of being sun-dried, as most Asiatic "brick" was and is, and was laid in a pattern well known today. The twin cities were built entirely of it— houses, city walls, the great citadel, the streets, the granaries, the temples, the baths, the approach ramps— though sun-dried brick was used as filler. So plentiful and durable is this brick that the ruins of Harappa have been badly despoiled over the years by brick-pickers who have carried it away by the cartload.

This universality of uniform brick laid in regular courses, and unrelieved by stone or wood or architectural ornament, imparts a look of monotonous rigidity and exactitude to the cities that is only reënforced when we look into their culture. Piggott says, "There is a terrible efficiency about the Harappa civilization which recalls all the worst of Rome." Every detail contributes to this summation. The twin cities are laid out on a grid plan of streets (some of them 30 feet wide) which divided them into 12 major blocks. The plastered walls of the close-set houses face the street blankly, unmarked by anything but a door. Perhaps these house walls were painted but very likely, considering the conservative nature of the Harappans and the kind of pigment available, they were all painted the same color. Behind the row of houses was a row of courts or "back yards," which were separated from the courts on the next street by alleyways. And when floods of the Indus River several times swept through Mohenjo-Daro it was rebuilt exactly as it had been before, every wall being precisely replaced in its previous position.

It is not surprising that the Harappans had the most exact system of measures and weights in the ancient world and that all structures were built not by eye but to dimension. Foot and cubit rulers have been found, engraved on bronze (the Harappan was a strictly Bronze Age civilization) and on shell. The foot was very close to our own, 13.2 inches, and the cubit was 20.62, both units conforming to those in use throughout the Near East. But nowhere else were they so standardized. Whether you were in Mohenjo-Daro or in Harappa, 400 miles away, a foot was a foot, 13.2 inches.

It goes without saying that items of wide usage like pottery were mass produced. In a way this is understandable. The Harappans apparently followed the ritual custom, now observed among the Hindus, of never drinking twice from the same cup. They needed to make a great many drinking cups. The grain, wheat and barley that fed the Harappan urban populace was ground not by each housewife to suit her own convenience but in large community mills. The grain itself was centrally stored in public granaries. And the metal-smelting furnaces were not those of individual smiths; they, too, were large industrial-type installations, manned by workers who were apparently not the artisans but mere production workers in raw material. This kind of arrangement is much less remarkable today than it was in the ancient world when such work was individual, and organized by crafts or guilds. The location of a sort of barracks near the mills and furnaces makes it almost certain that much of the common labor was done by slaves.

Archaeological digging, even in rich sites, is, like war, more monotonous than anything else. Even so, monotonously to excavate monotony, as at Harappa and Mohenjo-Daro, is to earn the occasional sidelight that, more than anything else, returns a vanished people to life. During the excavation of Chanhu-Daro, one of the minor Harappan habitation sites, a strange set of markings were discovered on a brick. When they were deciphered they turned out to be the tracks of a dog chasing a cat over the brick while it was still soft. And he hadn't caught her.

It takes just such a touch as this to shake us out of our feeling that the Harappans were a race of brick-faced robots. People who keep dogs and cats as pets, with the dogs chasing the cats and not catching them—such people are no more ancient than we are. Archaeology shows that for a thousand years nothing in Harappa changed, or was allowed to change. For a thousand years the tools did not change, the language did not change (at least as written), customs did not change, the government did not change. This we don't understand and we are prepared to forget Harappa. But cats and dogs and people who keep them for the pleasure and companionship they give are people fully capable of having done something that will interest us.

The story in a nutshell is that Harappa, much like Poverty Point, seems suddenly to appear on the landscape out of nothing that preceded it developmentally. As a civilization the Harappans seem to have had no childhood. When they are first encountered by the archaeologist they are living in their well-built cities and towns, their government so perfectly organized there is no need to change it, and so uniform that it could carry on from two capitals—Mohenjo-Daro and Harappa. There is a writing system of 400 characters, much more advanced than the early Sumerian. There is a Bronze Age technology—no old-fashioned flint tools for these workers. There is stone sculpture, sculpture in cast bronze and baked clay and a mature development of the engraving art, especially in the work done on seals; there was a jeweler's art. There were ox-drawn carts (excavation of the ruts left by their wheels show them to be of the same wheelbase used today in India) and a little ox-drawn vehicle with a roof and side curtains, a sort of surrey with the fringe on top. There was the ever-present gambling game, with the familiar spotted dice. There was a fine cotton-weaving industry; and there was trade, overland by pack animal, and overseas by sailing ship. The very list of items imported makes the Harappans sound exotically sophisticated: shells for inlays, alabaster and carnelian, agates and onyx, chalcedony, rock crystal, turquoise, silver, gold, lapis lazuli, jasper and bloodstone, and materials less expensive-sounding—steatite, slate, bitumen, lead, copper, tin and the red pigment hematite.

A thousand years is an almost inconceivably long time. We know only too well how much can happen in a thousand years. The year 1066, when William of Normandy invaded England, is only 900 years behind us but we feel that all we could possibly be expected to know and remember about history began that year.

But nothing happened in Harappa during an equal span. An Harappan of 4500 years ago resurrected 3500 years ago would never know he had been away. And this is what is remarkable about the Harappans. How did they do it? They were a literate, advanced, hardworking, competent people who could not only build a city but could plan it. Apparently they invented much of their own civilization and, except for the lack of science, it was a complete civilization, satisfying every need of its people at the time.

How they did it, on the available evidence, was by religion. Piggott points out over and over the Harappan practices that are those of the non-aggressive, contemplative, inward-looking Hindus of today. Undoubtedly the Harappans were regimented, but they must have wanted to be regimented. What they believed and did satisfied them wholely. This is as remarkable as the fact that they were energetic and progressive enough to have built a civilization yet, at a given point, stopped being progressive and never again learned anything or forgot anything. There can be only one answer to such a puzzle. Harappa owed its fast rise to a peak of civilization the equal of anything in the world, at the time, to the leadership of a few men of genius. When there were no more geniuses, there was no further progress.

It would not do to leave the Harappans without saying something about who they were. There was an element of the Proto-Australoid—that is, of the parent stock of the Australian Black Fellow—but there were few and apparently of an inferior caste. There was an occasional Mongoloid, or typical Asiatic. But a stronger strain was the round-headed Alpine and the dominant strain was the slight, dark, long-headed Mediterranean. In short, these were our old friends, the Neolithic Farmers. They are found everywhere from Western Asia to Ireland wherever agriculture begins.

And thus it seems that those wild lords of the central Euro-Asiatic plains, the Battle-Ax horsemen and stockmen, the spreaders of the Indo-European root language, have met the Neolithic Farmers at both ends of the line. It was because they had met the farmers at both ends of the line and all along it and had made their mark everywhere that they are called the Indo-Europeans. Geoffrey

Bibby, archaeologist and prehistorian, says that about 4000 years ago, at which time the Battle-Axers were reaching Denmark, their spread was the most important trend happening in the world. Though they razed Harappa and Mohenjo-Daro and destroyed urban civilization in India for generations to come, they seem not to have seriously interrupted the social-religious traditions that eventually became Hinduism and its mystical offshoots. What they contributed, in the final summing up, was a language.

That is what they contributed everywhere—a language that, for some reason or other, stamped out of existence any other language with which it met head-on. The Indo-Europeans cannot and must not be spoken of as though they were a race; that is, all of unmixed blood and physical characteristics. The Battle-Axers themselves were the Caucasian blond or red-haired, blue-eyed people who were born to the nomad life of the steppes and who retained some sort of loose tribal feeling of kinship for hundreds of years. When they left this environment for other lands it was not as a wave of conquering people sweeping all before them, but in smaller clanlike parties, infiltrating rather than decimating. From the beginning they seem to have taken their places as princes among the people of their new chosen land, not as conquering kings. Their blood was quickly intermixed with the older populations. But either because of the forcefulness of their personalities or something inherently appealing in their language, it was the language that grew and spread and became dominant, rather than the genetic elements of the Battle-Axers.

Because it was never written down nobody knows what the Indo-European root language was. Linguists only know what it was like; but languages deriving from it carry all that burden of knowledge and thought which has become known as Western Civilization and of which we, as Americans, are a part.

14

Men of the Stone Age

WE ARE ABOUT to cross a boundary, into the real Stone Age.

Up to now we have been probing into what we have previously called and still think of, as modern prehistory; that is, prehistory which begins with the first practice of farming, and its inevitable consequence, villages and a settled, permanent community life. Out of this grew civilization.

We are prepared to cross that boundary where the races, languages and way of life have only the remotest relation to us. That relation is, however, one of common humanity. The men of the Stone Age kept the human race alive and thriving and increasingly dominant as a species of animal among hundreds of species more numerous or more powerful.

Except for writing and the method of food production called husbandry, these men of the Old Stone Age first did most of what we now regard as the human things to do: they began religious ritual and held the first notions about a supernatural Being; they made the first tools and thought up all the basic tool ideas; they painted, some of them beautifully, and sculpted in stone and ivory; they invented narration, the basis for all our imaginative literature, as is evident from the universal occurrence of pre-literate myths and tales; in a sense, they invented themselves. For, in the course of a half million years, they made themselves over from an instinctive animal to a thinking one.

We have already crossed the boundary between the Stone Age and "modern" prehistory in references to the almost-villages of Wapanucket No. 6 and the Pickwick Basin shell mounds. What that boundary is must by now be clear— the line between the production of food by planting, cultivation and harvesting of plant foods and the management of meat animals on the one hand and the mere harvesting, by the techniques of hunting, fishing and gathering of the plant and animal foods nature produces, on the other.

The Neolithic or New Stone Age was the first age of farming and so was not really of the Stone Age, though it was the last age during which, in cultural evolution, stone was a principal stock material for tools. The last full Stone Age, economically and materially, was the Mesolithic; that is Middle Stone Age, so called because it stands between the Neolithic and the Paleolithic, or Old Stone Age.

In our reference to the coming of the Neolithic farmers to Britain mention was made of a native population of hunters. These are known in British archaeology as the Peterborough folk. So confirmed were they in their hunting habits that they went on living strictly as hunters and gatherers for hundreds of years along the lakes and marshes, unconverted to the advantages of farming. There was then plenty of room for everybody. This kind of coexistence of hunter and farmer happened all over Europe, until the Stone Age faded from the scene as farmers and herdsmen took over the land and narrowed down the territory for such living.

These Peterborough people were the original Britons. They were the descendants of the Mesolithic hunters who were the occupants of Britain when it became an island, about 8,000 years ago. Until then it had been but a peninsula of Europe, like Italy, and any people who were so inclined could have walked from Land's End in Cornwall all the way across Europe, Asia, and into Alaska, which was almost certainly then still connected by land bridge to Asia.

Two or three distinct cultural groups made their way north with the forests and west through the bog country.

Two of them were the Tardenoisians and Azilians. The former brought with them the first domesticated dogs and both made very small geometric flint tools. These people came from France and ultimately from Africa. They were petering out when they reached England.

A third seasonal wandering Mesolithic people with whom we are about to be concerned are called the Maglemosians—The Big Bog people—because their remains have been excavated most frequently from bogs. This occurrence is not because these people lived amphibiously in bogs but because the shores of the ancient lakes about which they lived have become bogs since then. The first and most numerous finds were in Denmark (Maglemosian is a Danish word) but the latest and probably best excavated Maglemosian site is on a bog edge near Star Carr, Yorkshire, England.

These Maglemosians best represent the Mesolithic cultures because they represent the best adaptation to the climatic environmental conditions of the time. As the last great glacier retreated—in Europe it was the Wurm —it left behind vast planed areas which were just right for the growth of grass. Enormous herds of edible animals including the mammoth and the horse waxed fat on these pastures and Paleolithic hunters waxed fat on the herds.

But the climate continued to warm and forests began to take over the land—first the pines and evergreens and then the birches and finally the hard woods. Their grazing lands gone, the big herds were doomed to extinction.

The new game animals were forest-dwellers and their herds were small. Entirely new methods of hunting and a new lore of living were required to stay alive. The Maglemosians developed this lore, and its pattern reminds us very much of the kind of life lived by our woodland Amerinds before they began to raise corn, beans and squash.

Thus the Mesolithic is more than just a change in styles of tool-making, of which the most distinctive is the microlith technique; it is a whole new way of life adjusted to new climatically-dictated hunting and gathering circumstances. The C14 date on the Star Carr site is about 9500 years ago. On the Fairbridge chart this is a time of increasing warmth and rise of sea level until about 8500 years ago, when the sea was within perhaps 40 feet of its present level. But at the time of the Star Carr site occupation the weather had just turned and the sea was about 85 feet below its present level. The climate was warming in England, but it was still only as warm as present-day Canada, and what is now the English Channel was a low country full of bogs but still above water. Star Carr is on the edge of this bog or, as the English call it, fen country, and is on the shore of one of the shallow lakes of that time, though the lake has since vanished.

The excavation, reported in the 1950s by J. G. D. Clark, who participated in it, suffered the disadvantages and gained the advantages of a water-logged site. The trenches were always half full of water, but the sodden sub-surface conditions had preserved a great deal of bone, antler, wood and vegetation. It had only to hold together long enough for restorative measures to be taken. As a result the Star Carr site appears to be the oldest in Europe where such quantities and kinds of perishable material were recovered.

Though the Star Carr site is small, about 2,000 square feet in area, it was an actual settlement, probably occupied seasonally by an extended family. This would consist of the surviving grandparents, their sons, the sons' daughters and the daughters' husbands. Hunting, especially woodland hunting, cannot support large groups of people in one locale, since a large group very quickly uses up the available food. But too small a group would not be able to support itself. Dependent largely on its adult male hunters for food, the band must number enough of these so that it can survive if one or two are incapacitated. Even a small band cannot stay too long in one place. The band that made Star Carr its camp must have had other camps, perhaps three or four, which it considered equally to be "home."

The principal feature at the Star Carr site, the one which gives it a unique interest, is a platform or flooring of birch poles, weighed down with clay and stones and laid on the soft mud of the lake shore. Presumably it was meant to be walked on and probably to support shelters. No evidence remained to show what these shelters might have been like. Since hide-working flints were found in the Star Carr mud, the shelters may have

The oldest man-felled tree yet discovered as it lies in the archaeologist's excavation trench. Star Carr, Yorkshire, England.

been of skin, like the tipis of our American plains Indians. Or they might have been the kind of bark-covered frame wigwams used by our eastern forest Indians. There was plenty of birch bark to be had for this purpose.

Crooked, water-soaked-rotten, mud-slimed, these Star Carr platform poles will have their place in a museum for years to come. At present they are the oldest ax-cut logs in the world. Wood is a wonderful material and man has leaned heavily on it throughout his career, but it is of only minor use until he has an ax to cut down trees. The early Maglemosians of Star Carr used a type of light ax or adze which they re-sharpened again and again by clipping the edge. The platform logs were cut neatly all around to a point, like a sharpened pencil. This is not at all the way a woodsman cuts through a tree with a steel ax.

But this was not the extent of wood cutting at Star Carr. Among the perishable material recoveries was part of a wooden paddle, the world's oldest piece of navigation equipment. No boat was found, but had one been it would most likely have been a dugout canoe. Primitive rafts and canoe-like boats have been made of reeds, however, as well as of skins.

The Star Carr band was prepared, then, to exploit the resources of the lake it probably regarded as its own. Fish bones were absent—too fragile to survive, no doubt —but one probable fishing harpoon head came out of the muck, and the bones of beaver and at least five kinds of water fowl have been identified amongst the skeletal leavings. A painstakingly thorough analysis of these leavings makes it clear how versatile these Maglemosians were, and had to be. Living on the shore of their lake, they were also living on the "shore" of the forest, and they lived off both, probably in nearly equal ratio.

The red deer was the staple meat animal. Not only were its bones most numerous (the bones of 160 individuals were found) but, when these bones were calculated for actual meat carried, it was found responsible for more "take-home" meals than all other game animals combined, furnishing about 67,000 pounds of meat. The roe deer had also been killed in large numbers—the bones of 66 individuals were found—but had furnished only about 2400 pounds of meat. The forest ox was the prime meat producer per individual—18 individuals had produced about 18,000 pounds of meat—but not enough of them, probably not more than one or two a season, fell to the Star Carr hunters.

Among the tools recovered were specimens of a kind of mattock made of elk antler. Whatever it is called it is undoubtedly a grubbing or digging tool, the one purpose of which, among these people, would have been to harvest edible roots in order to add carbohydrates to a diet that leaned heavily on proteins. The harvesting of any above-ground edible leaf, nut, berry or stalk within hand reach is taken for granted.

It was calculated by the archaeological team at Star Carr that the total amount of meat known from skeletal material to have been furnished for the Star Carr camp would have served to feed the band for about six years. From these remains it has been deduced that the camp was set here during late winter and early spring. Assuming that not by any means all of the skeletal material was recovered (part of the site was dry, and all perishable material had perished) and noting that no fish bones were recovered and that there is no way of calculating how much vegetal food was consumed, we can safely conclude that Star Carr was a band headquarters for at least a decade.

Cozy is not the word for this kind of life; neither is miserable. It was a busy life, with little leisure from the constant round of food seeking; and it was a life that permitted few mistakes in either judgment or action. There were no stores to resort to, if the hunt failed and no carcass was brought home for meat and for the hide needed for clothing. A man who broke a tool had to make himself another. Whatever damage was done by weather or misadventure had to be repaired by the man himself, out of materials he had to find and shape.

On the other hand there must have been many a day, even many a season, during which a Star Carr hunter could have looked about him with content. The band had its shelters and its clothing—not simple skin blankets, but shaped garments—it had wood for the fire, the flint and "steel" (iron pyrites) to light that fire at will, and possibly night light.

Recovered from the Star Carr site were several rolls of birch bark. No evidence was discovered of the kind of sewing used to make bark baskets of this material, or to attach it to anything as roofing, and it was decided that the rolls had been gathered for boiling down for the resin. This resin becomes a pitch and was used to attach weapon and tool points to shafts. (Among our northern American forest Indians there was another reason for gathering birch bark into short, tight rolls. Because of the resin, they made excellent torches.)

This Maglemosian Mesolithic band at Star Carr becomes more and more familiar to us the more we compare it with our forest, particularly our northern forest Indians. Their use of the bow drill to perforate pebbles for beads was widely practiced, and their manufacture of antler headdresses reminds us both of Hopewellian shaman headdress and the camouflage used by historic Indians for game stalking. Nor is the microlithic technique, at which the Star Carr flintsmiths were so proficient, nor the burin, a specialized antler working tool, foreign to America.

Though flintsmithing might seem a relatively simple matter of knocking one stone against another, a book the size of this one could be written on the subject of the manufacture of stone tools. Microlithic technique would take up a whole chapter. What it consists of is knocking off the bulbous end of a pebble so that a flat surface, called a striking platform, is left for the flint knapper to work on. He strikes downward all along the edge of this flat surface with sharp, but not smashing, blows. If his strike is properly gauged the flake struck off runs the length of the pebble and comes off as a blade, with straight, parallel-sided edges, both of which are razor sharp.

What is so great about this? Only that it is against the nature of flint to break this way. It wants to spall off in coin-shaped chips which, though sharp-edged all around, do not make very good tool forms. That is, they do not make good tool forms when man wants to specialize his tools. For a couple of hundred thousand years these round chips were mankind's only knife and they always retained a certain casual utility whenever struck off.

Eventually, however, the idea dawned that the shape of the flake could be controlled. The first recognized controlled chip is called the Levallois Flake. It is not really a flake but a whole tool. A core was prepared with a striking platform and then the tool was shaped on the core. It had to be a fairly simple shape, of course. Then the tool thus shaped was struck off the core at one blow and was ready for use. Later these "flakes" began to be retouched and shaped into more specialized tools.

It is not at all a far cry from the Levallois Flake to the blade technique. The earliest blades are macro (great) blades, and have been struck off as much as nine inches long. They look like petrified swords. The trend to smaller or micro blades may have had several causes, but one thing is clear: when the stone tool ceased to be the whole tool and became part of a tool, being set into a handle or a shaft, then the blade size was reduced. The reduction went on, doubtless, until the minimum usable size had been reached.

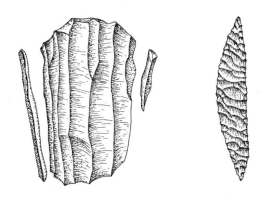

STRIP-BLADE CORE AND RETOUCHED TOOL

The tool to the right was made from a blade-like flake struck from the core at left. It takes considerable skill to strike off these strip blades from a stone core, which must be prepared in advance for this technique.

Whenever burins are discovered at a site it is beyond question that the inhabitants of that site worked antler or ivory. The burin is a bone-working tool and for antler and ivory it is indispensable. The edge of a flint chip is sharp but brittle and, used on tough substances like ivory or antler or even bone and hard wood, loses its edge too quickly for efficiency. The burin is a tool with a cutting edge like a chisel, sharp at the edge but thick immediately behind. It can be re-sharpened by striking off a single tiny blade. It was, in the Stone Age, as much an artist's as an artisan's tool.

At Star Carr its employment was utilitarian only, and it made possible the utilization of the plentiful antler

THE ENGRAVER'S TOOL

These three tools are all forms of the burin, used to cut or engrave bone, or to engrave stone.

from deer and elk so that this material almost reached the popularity of flint. Long, narrow splinters burined out of an antler tine and converted into barbed weapon points were one of the most numerous finds, as would be expected at a hunting camp.

What we find at Star Carr, to sum up, is a people who can show the ax and, perhaps, the mattock as the Mesolithic contribution to mankind's progress. Undoubtedly there was more that we will never know about, all the knowledge of a forested world the Maglemosians had acquired from living in it successfully. While their technology was mainly an inheritance from the Paleolithic they had the resource to adapt it to the very environment that killed off the Paleolithic.

But it must be pointed out that in perhaps the same decade, or the same century that early Maglemosian

182

people occupied the Star Carr camp site, agriculture may
have begun at Karim Shahir, in the vicinity of Jarmo.
Some 5000 years later, when the Neolithic Farmers
brought agriculture to Britain, the Peterborough people
they found there were still Mesolithic hunters whose
only acquired new trait was pottery, and not very good
pottery.

It can be argued that the people of the Mesolithic Age,
though succeeding the Paleolithic, did not progress beyond it. Except, of course, as one group of Mesolithic
people in one locality. In very few places did the old
Mesolithic hunters become farmers. They followed the
life they loved to the end. And so it was and is, in the
main, with our American Indians. Very few of them
cared for the civilization they were offered—or threatened with.

15

The Mammoth Killers

IN NORTH AMERICA the last or Wisconsin glaciation reached its climax and most extensive coverage of the land, according to Fairbridge and others, at about 17,000 years ago. At that time it had invaded as far south as Long Island, opposite New York City, and, farther west, lay within 50 miles of the Ohio River. The European equivalent of the Wisconsin, called the Würm, is regarded as being generally synchronized in its movements with the Wisconsin, which was vastly larger. The late Paleolithic period of Europe starts with the decline of the Würm glaciation and extends to that time when forests took root and changed the living habits of man.

This distinction is not a matter of convenience. When the Würm-Wisconsin stood at its maximum, the level of the world ocean was at least 320 feet below where it is now, according to Fairbridge, and as much as 400 feet lower according to others. It takes very little imagination to understand that a map of the world at that time had to be far different from what it is now. Africa and Europe were separated not so much by geography as by climate.

Even as this late Paleolithic world was geographically and climatically different from our world, so was its animal life. Mammoth and musk ox, the bison, the reindeer, the elk, the horse, among the herd animals and the cave bear and the cave lion, along with the wolf and the leopard, were the real owners of the landscape. But man himself was different, in the Old World at least. Old Neanderthal—he who has come to be known as The Cave Man, with his short, crooked-legged stance and his brow-ridged, rough-hewn face, he who had so well adapted himself to the frigidity of a glaciated world with his fire and cave-dwelling—Old Neanderthal faded away, as the mammoth was soon about to do. In some places he was exterminated by his enemies, in others he simply died out, while in still others he mated with a new breed and exists today only in the profile and physique of an occasional individual. The late Paleolithic is the time of the establishment of modern *Homo sapiens*, as the earth's dominant human species.

All along the rim of the Würm glacier—from Land's

End, across France and Germany, and into Russia—extended the Great Plain. It was a zone of tundra, the natural habitat of mammoth, musk ox and reindeer.

(Of these three species, only the mammoth is extinct today. But we know as much about him as we could know if he were alive, except, possibly, what he smelled like. This is because mammoths, weighing tons, occasionally broke through thin ice, were drowned, and their bodies then frozen and preserved until modern times. Whole mammoths in the flesh have been found in Alaska. But the most famous survivor is the mammoth from the Bereskova River in Siberia. He died after a hearty meal, was immediately refrigerated, and when he melted out of his icy tomb, the meal was still in his stomach, undigested. It consisted of Alpine poppy, wild thyme, crow's foot and several of the grasses that go to make up a tundra vegetation. What a live mammoth smells like we don't know, but we do know that a dead one smells awful.)

At the Russian end of the Central European Plain, men who were first cousins to the Cro-Magnons—that very tall (the men averaged six feet) very modern-looking race which is credited with exterminating the Neanderthals—found a way to kill mammoths and to make their killing into a very prosperous subsistence. At the western end of the Central Plain the Cro-Magnons and their successors made a similarly good living off the herds of horses and reindeer. So dependent were these late Paleolithic hunters on the reindeer for meat, antlers, hides and shelter that in Western Europe the late Paleolithic is called the Reindeer Age.

Though this period of the waning of the Würm-Wisconsin glaciation was probably the most animal-rich of the earth's long faunal history, there had always been plenty of meat, had man been able to take it. Now he was, and the yield was such that he had, for the first time, leisure to work for something besides his stomach. Now man the artist enters the scene and a great art begins to appear on the walls of caves. This is not art as we know, done for the sake of its inherent beauty and expressed substance. It is an art related to magic and social and religious ritual. But it is art, just the same. The human hand-brain-eye combination, trained by hundreds of thousands of years of tool-making and use, is here turned to the representation of the things of the world around it and, regardless of the motive, the expression is as fine as anything our civilized artists could have achieved then, or could achieve now.

Stimulated and freed by the food abundance created by climatological conditions, late Paleolithic man created the Golden Age of the hunter. Even as he achieved a fine art of his own, so did he become the complete artisan, both in his ability to work stone, bone, antler and elephant ivory and in his creation of new tool ideas, including the spear-thrower (in America called the atlatl), the bow, the recoverable harpoon and the burin. Technologically this was the day of blade-making. It was the day of the eyed needle and sewn, shaped or "tailored" clothing. It was the day when man learned to make fire by flint and pyrites and, probably, by other means. It was the first day of trade relations, by barter of course, and it may have been, after the extinction of the Neanderthals, the last centuries of peace in Europe. The Russian mammoth killers and the western Cro-Magnons, whose remains have been found as far west as England, were of one culture, and almost certainly of one blood and race. There is no evidence of violence among them.

While this game-rich period of late Wisconsin-Würm times in Europe has found its way readily enough into publication, the same period in America is very little known because it has only lately become known. The herds of mammoth and ancient bison (much larger than Buffalo Bill's buffalo), of horse and camel, were immensely larger than the herds that fed on the Central European Plain. They could roam from Canada to the Valley of Mexico, and from the Rockies to western New York and Alabama. But our Amerind mammoth hunters never reached the same level of achievement as their European cousins. Nevertheless, they have left on the record the greatest single feat of hunting that archaeology is ever likely to reveal.

To kill a mammoth—a huge, active herd animal—by any means must be considered a large exploit. To stalk a full-grown mammoth in the prime of life armed with nothing but a stone-tipped spear and to kill him with that spear is surely unsurpassable. And that is exactly what a band of Clovis spearmen did about 9500 years ago near what is now Naco, Arizona, very close to the Mexican border.

In numbers known to have been killed on archaeological evidence, the European counterparts of the Amerinds were the greatest of all mammoth killers. The bones of about 900 mammoths have been counted from the Prêdmost site, near a pass through the mountains that connected the Russian with the Hungarian plains. In addition there was plentiful skeletal material of the horse, musk ox, bison and reindeer. But among the thousands of flint and bone tools there was nothing resembling a weapon that might have killed a mammoth; or any of the other beasts taken as game.

The Prêdmost mammoth-killers had not been hunters as we think of hunters—pursuers of a quarry which they intend to kill through the accuracy of their marksmanship with a deadly weapon. In the first place the majority of mammoth bones at Prêdmost were those of animals too young or too old—too young to take care of themselves or too old to get around much any more. These must have been lured into straying from the herd or were not able to keep up with the crowd as it pushed through the pass from winter pasture in the south to summer pasture in the north. Then, when the circumstances were right, groups of mammoths were probably driven into pit traps or into bogs or over cliffs. This kind of slaughter drive has been used the world over to take herd animals. "Buffalo jumps," that is, cliffs over which the Plains bison were stampeded, often by fire, and at the base of which bones lie to this day in tangled heaps, are common in our West.

Were it not for the find at Naco, the weapon-killing of a beast the size of a mammoth by Stone Age Man would be widely doubted. This would not be a matter of stubborn skepticism. The mammoth, bulking as large as the African elephant or larger, in the case of the American imperial mammoth, cannot be reached in a vital spot by anything short of an express rifle. In prime condition he would be protected by a layer of fat a foot thick. The sheer physical impossibility of driving a spear into the heart of a mammoth must have been evident from the moment the first carcass was butchered. But there is a spot—it might almost be called a secret spot— where an unerringly aimed stone-headed spear, thrown with sufficient force, can kill a mammoth as dead as need be. And how the Amerind hunter found it we will never know.

Stone spearheads have been found, in America, inside the rib cages of the now extinct form of Plains buffalo called Taylor's bison, a species about a quarter larger than the historic buffalo. The location of these finds certainly leads to the conclusion that the Amerind hunters of 10,000 years ago were trying for the vitals and had every intention of perpetrating a kill by weapon.

Archaeologists try to stay clear of reading the minds of men of 10,000 years ago and they usually prefer to interpret the spearhead-inflicted injuries in another way.

Stampedes by fire and other means of startlement were useful on herds. The single animal would be hounded toward his doom by other means; that is, by the hunting party harassing it from the rear with missiles, including spears. These would not be cast with the expectation of killing but only of keeping the beast fleeing and heading into a swamp from which it could not flounder its way out, or toward a cliff it would see too late.

In the case of the two mammoths excavated at Santa Isabel Iztapan in the Valley of Mexico within two years of each other, this is obviously the case. They were found about 500 yards apart, one in 1952 and one in 1954, on what was probably, at the time, the shores of Lake Texcoco, now greatly shrunk in the drier, hotter weather of later eras.

There was one spearhead in the first Iztapan mammoth and there were two in the second, none of them in the mammoth's known vulnerable spot. That there had been kills in both instances were ascertained by the presence also on the site of tools for cutting off the meat and from the fact that scars on the bones had been made by these cutting tools. The discovery of two mammoths so close together under exactly the same circumstances established beyond doubt that Amerinds had lived (1) with the mammoth, (2) off the mammoth, that is, mammoth flesh and (3) they hunted individual mammoths and must therefore have hunted them in small bands.

The evidence of Iztapan would lead nobody to suspect

that a mammoth would ever be found spear-killed. The likelihood was that probably several other spears had been cast into the mammoths and had been thriftily retrieved. Those found by the excavators (Luis Avelcyra A. DeAnda and Manuel Maldonado Koerdell) had probably been lost or forgotten by the hunters or were not retrievable. No single hunter or pair of hunters would ever have tried to bag a mammoth. But however numerous the hunters were, the wounds they inflicted had not been lethal of themselves, though they must have bled the mammoths and hastened their deaths by exhaustion.

To see what can really be done with a spear we have to go to the Naco site excavated by Emil W. Haury. The bones of the Naco mammoth were first noticed by Fred and Marc Navarrete (father and son), who saw them sticking out of the edge of Greenbush Creek after a rain storm. The two Navarettes, interested in archaeology, began the excavation themselves. But as soon as they found two projectile points which they were well enough informed to know were of a very early "fluted" type, they sent to the Arizona State Museum for Dr. Haury's help.

(A word must be inserted here about what "fluted" spear points are. They are found all over North America and are indicative of hunting Amerinds of about 9000 years ago or longer. They are lanceolate in form and are named from the fact that a long flute or channel flake, much like the "blades" we have described, is struck from

Disinterment of the Naco (Arizona) mammoth. The excavator in the upper left-hand corner has uncovered two teeth.

the bottom so that it leaves a groove up the face of the point. This may be done on one or both sides and one, two or three flakes may be taken out to make the groove for the point's insertion into the split end of the spear shaft. There can be little doubt about this because both edges of the point were dulled by grinding approximately the length of the groove so as not to cut the binding by which the point was fastened to the shaft. This point is called Clovis fluted, from the Clovis, New Mexico, site where it was first recognized. It is almost always found with mammoth kills, whereas its better-made cousin, the Folsom fluted, is almost always found with kills of extinct bison. These fluted points, which are a strictly early Amerind type, have not been found, so far, on sites less than 9000 years old and have been found archaeologically only in America. They are, needless to say, a highly prized artifact.)

The Naco mammoth was excavated with all manner of experts on hand to scrutinize every fact pertaining to it. John F. Lance was there as paleontologist to study the mammoth skeleton itself. He discovered it to be a mature or nearly mature specimen. The geology expert was Ernest Antevs, an acknowledged authority on the land formations of the West. It was he who determined that while the mammoth had died on the edge of a creek, he had not been mired down in soft mud but had been standing on firm sand.

So this was no kill like the Iztapan mammoths, nor had the prey of the Naco hunters been the easy calf or the doddering bull. Nor had the Naco spearmen, it was stunningly clear when Haury completed the archaeology, cast their shafts merely to put a little get-up-and-go into the mammoth's rump.

Eight Clovis points were taken out of the mammoth's scattered skeleton. Two of them had been removed by the Navarretes; one had slipped out of place and was found in the dirt; five were found in the undisturbed positions in which they had been held by the dirt for more than 9000 years.

They had all, it was determined by Haury, been in the target area of that one place where a mammoth can suffer a fatal wound from a spear. This is the atlas vertebra, high in the neck, just behind the head, and it sticks up in an exposed position. These Naco spearmen

Courtesy of the Arizona State Museum

These eight Clovis fluted projectile points were found within the "target" area of the Naco mammoth. The point at bottom left, probably carried the fatal thrust into the mammoth's spinal cord.

had known exactly what they were doing when they took as their bull's-eye this spot ten feet off the ground and, to the naked eye, just a lump of bone. Not only had all eight shafts hit in the target area but one point had hit the atlas vertebra dead center and had split it.

Perhaps the mammoth died technically of strangulation or some other inability to function. But one thing is certain, he could not have gone on living and moving with his spinal cord cut. You couldn't ask for a cleaner kill, and for it to have been so responsibly discovered and so expertly excavated is one of the luckiest finds in archaeology.

Undoubtedly this had been an ambush at a waterhole. Eight spearmen must have risen from their covert simultaneously, probably without even needing a signal, and had let fly their volley with one concerted aim. They must have known immediately that they had got their quarry, for he could not have moved much with a split backbone. They did not waste any more spears on him, or at least they did not leave any others in the body.

But this may be looked at another way. Let us suppose that the reason the eight points were found was because they were all in the target area. When the mammoth fell, eight spear shafts pointing up from his neck, each man who had cast one of those shafts had left it there as (1) a demonstration of his prowess and (2) the sign of his right to claim a share of the choicest portions. Thus, perhaps man's pride and sense of property may have given us a unique archaeological discovery. This is only right, for such things are as archaeological as man's artifacts. It just happens that they are much less often preserved.

Numbering eight such spearmen, this must have been a powerful hunting band. We can almost count them, the wives and children, and one or two old men no longer able to hunt. This would be a band not much different in size from that which frequented Star Carr, perhaps 25 to 30 persons. Perhaps the eight spears do not represent eight able-bodied spearmen, but this seems the likeliest interpretation—that eight shafts were launched at the same time from the same spot, to which the drinking mammoth presented the same target. By no means the only possible explanation, it does fit the excavated situation. No small, weak party would have chosen a mature but young and vigorous beast for attack.

A less dramatic water-hole site of mammoth-killing by Clovis spearmen, but one more productive in the number and kinds of beasts slain, was excavated by Haury in 1956 at the Lehner Ranch, also in Arizona, near Hereford about 12 miles from the Naco site. Bones of nine calf and young adult mammoths, horse, bison and tapir were taken out of a bank, much like the situation at Naco, near a watering-hole in a stream now being appropriately called Mammoth Kill Creek. The Naco team of Haury, Antevs and Lance, with the addition of the archaeologist E. B. Sayles, worked on this ancient scene of man's activity. Campfire charcoal yielded C14 dates of between 11,000 and 12,000 years ago, plus 13 Clovis points and 8 butchering tools.

Nothing as decisive as a spearhead in an atlas vertebra turned up, though two points were touching vertebrae and one was in the head. What did occur was plenty of confirming evidence of the hunting habits of the Clovis-point-making Amerind hunter of the period that in the Old World is called the late Paleolithic. Haury believes that the same people, possibly the same hunting band, made the kills at both Naco and the Lehner Ranch. The charcoal for dating the Lehner site was obtained from two well defined hearths, but that for Naco had to be gathered in crumbs scattered through the sands. The latter was not satisfactory, then, and the date of 9300 years ago that it gave is the less preferred. The Lehner site was dated by several runs of C14 at an age best placed at 11,500 years ago. But Antevs believes both sites to be about 13,000 years old. It must be borne carefully in mind that when charcoal is exposed to the weather and vegetation in open sites it can become contaminated by more recent carbon 14 and this will give the run a younger result.

What these campfires at Mammoth Kill Creek and the scattered charcoal at Naco tell us is that the Clovis spearmen regularly ambushed their game at waterholes, dropped them there, and camped at the spot of the kill. The ability of the hunters to hold the game where attacked is important. It saved many a weary mile of tracking after wounded game, waiting for it to drop or losing it to wolves or one of the carnivorous killers—the saber-tooth tiger or the American lion, now called the American jaguar, about 25% larger than the African lion. The choice of juvenile mammoths for attack does not weigh against the courage of the Clovis hunters. These were the juicy and tender "veal" animals. What tells for their courage is that the attack was close-in, against an animal that, though it was probably trapped by high creek banks, was not bogged down or otherwise immobile.

Haury thinks the Mammoth Kill Creek waterhole was hunted periodically, but over a period not longer than a year. The rotting carcasses would probably have fouled the location, no matter how quickly scavengers moved in to clean up, and after a while this hole would have been shunned by even the thirstiest game. There must have been other holes in the creek. The Naco and Lehner sites must have been repeated a thousand times over the rich savannah land of Arizona when climate and rainfall pattern made it as favorable a territory for herd animals as ever was the Central European Plain. For we are now fairly sure of this: the Clovis spearman hunted mammoths for at least 3000 years, and there were more than enough of these, until their mysterious extinction about 9000 years ago, to feed all the men in America.

It looks very much, therefore, as though the reason there was no flowering of man during the game-abundant post-glacial period in America was the manner of hunting. The material and artistic culture of the herd hunters of mammoth and later of buffalo shows no improvement over a matter of 5000 and probably 10,000 years. Why? Because they were men of the chase. They did not "harvest" meat from the herds and then take their leisure while they enjoyed the harvest. They hunted, with the greatest efficiency and daring, the single kill, and this kind of life, going from kill to kill, almost from meal to meal, so satisfied them, or kept them so busy, that it is impossible to find a single contribution they made to Amerind progress. When the heyday of the great herd beasts was over, so was theirs, and they died without legacy. Even their very fine work in flint, confined to point and knife forms, was not copied and never became a later Amerind tradition.

16

The Desert Culture People

THE CLOVIS MAMMOTH HUNTERS are only half the story of the America of 10,000 years ago. If they left nothing behind them, then who did?

The best representatives of the kind of hunting-gathering pattern of life as contrasted with the Clovis specialized mammoth hunters are the people of Danger Cave, Utah. They have been C14 dated at 11,000 years ago and hence must have been, by that determination, contemporaries of the mammoth hunters. You could hardly believe it after a comparison of the two cultures. Almost nothing survives in the open sites of the mammoth hunters. But in the three caves near Wendover, Utah, called Danger, Juke Box and Raven, what was excavated leads to the question of whether the mammoth hunters and the people called by archaeologists of the West the Desert Culture inhabited the same world.

And they did, indeed, live in different worlds. The Arizona habitat of the mammoth was still grassland crossed with streams, like Greenbush and Mammoth Kill creeks, but the Great Basin area of Nevada, Colorado, eastern California and Idaho was already beginning to feel the effects of insufficient rainfall. And it was the people who lived under harsh desert conditions and not those who lived off the mammoth fat of the land who were the most advanced.

Quite obviously it is hard to predict what human beings will do. If conditions are too harsh, then there is little time and opportunity left over from staying alive to think, plan, express oneself and thus advance toward a fuller humanity. When people cannot afford to make a mistake, then they cannot afford to experiment, to take chances. The result is a standing still, a static conservatism.

On the other hand, prosperity can likewise lead to smug and unprogressive conservatism. The Harappans were like this. So, it seems from our point of view, were the Clovis hunters and, perhaps, the Maglemosians. They were all hard working, competent, and even ingenious people, successful in their time and place. But unprepared to succeed beyond it.

What we must conclude is that the human race has progressed along a line in which periods of adversity and prosperity have to alternate. Success leads, eventually, to failure. But failure, or the threat of failure, stimulates to success. There were mammoths for the

EARLY HUNTERS' POINTS

At left is a Sandia point, found in a camel's bone in the excavation of Sandia Cave, New Mexico. In the center is a Clovis fluted point, used against the extinct mammoth, found at Clovis, New Mexico and other places. At right is a Gypsum Cave point, used against the extinct sloth, dated at about 10,000 years ago.

Clovisians and bison for the Folsoms to hunt long after the people of the Great Basin had to turn to other means to keep themselves in business. If, in truth, they ever had been big game hunters.

It seems more than possible that some of them never had been hunters. One of the oldest C14 dates in America is for a site at Tule Springs, Nevada. At first dated at more than 23,000 years ago, the datable material not being sufficient for a final determination, it has more recently been found, on further testing, to be more than 28,500 years old. Bones of camel, the extinct American horse and mammoth were found at Tule Springs, without spear points and with only the barest kind of "knives," the cutting edges of stone flakes, to cut off the meat.

The only possible interpretation is that the Tule Springs people were not spear hunters. They were coyote-like scavengers living off the calves and colts, the over-aged beasts, and cleaning up the leavings of the carnivore-killers, the big cats. They lived by the accidents that happened to individual animals. They could not cause "accidents" with the certainty that the spearmen could. Since they had to wait for accidents to happen and the wait might be long and hungry, they had to learn to fill in these waits with anything edible in sight. Sheer necessity taught them the uses of every plant and the way to bag every animal that inhabited their neighborhood.

When the climate turned against the Great Basin as pastureland, and the spearmen who were committed to the herd-hunting way of life vanished with the herds, the Desert Culture people probably never even noticed. They had, over the thousands of years since the scavenging days of Tule Springs, so developed their pattern of living that the herds had no place in it.

The Wendover Caves, of which Danger Cave proved the richest, were excavated in 1950–51 by Jesse D. Jennings. Half a dozen other caves in the Great Basin confirm Jennings' findings there. At 11,000 years ago the Desert Culture people showed signs of making that breakthrough from hunting into food production which heads men toward civilization. But it didn't quite happen. We will never know why it didn't. We can suspect it was lack of an individual genius to take the necessary last, important step. Primitive peoples always recognize such genius, it seems. They weave myths about them and freely accord them the credit due, although the myth usually takes over and hides the man. Anthropologists call such geniuses of myth "culture heroes" because their renown comes from wresting from some enemy a great good for their people. (Prometheus, whom the Greeks regarded as the giver of fire to mankind, was a culture hero.)

The basic advance made by the Desert Culture was the harvesting and hand milling of seeds by mano and metate to make meal for mush and meal cake. Both manos (or handstones), with which seeds of many kinds (the pickleweed being very important) were ground, and metates (the slab bottom half of the combination) are found in the lowest level of Danger Cave, C14 dated at about 11,000 years ago. Some 530 milling stones and 242 manos were found throughout the five levels, dated up to about A.D. 20. Jennings has reasonably concluded that the dwellers in Danger Cave were a band of extended family size—20 to 30 persons—and that the season of occupation was late summer and early autumn,

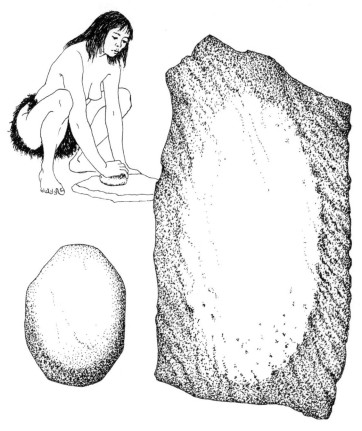

MANO AND METATE

This Desert Culture homemaker is grinding seeds into flour or meal with two grinding stones, a pebble mano (Spanish for hand) stone, and a free-stone slab metate.

when the pickleweed crop was harvested and the seeds parched as well as milled.

What must be recognized, nevertheless, is that on this time level the Danger Cave people were as culturally advanced—which does not mean quite the same thing as prosperous—as any human group. They were extraordinarily ingenious at getting the most out of their environment while living with utmost intimacy in it. Among the numerous finds in the Wendover Caves are over 1000 quids—masses of chewed material, like to-bacco quids. There were not quids of tobacco but of the leaves and underground shoots of the desert bulrush. Tobacco chewing is an unlovely habit but there is, sur-prisingly enough, a sanitary and healthful reason for it, aside from the narcotic effects. In atmospheres where there is much dust and heat a chewing cud keeps the mouth both moist, clean and refreshed. Chewing-gum is the currently acceptable cud, but it is not as good for this purpose as plant material.

The bulrush quids or cuds of the Desert Culture had all the absorbent effect of tobacco and were nutritional besides. An experimenter chewed a bulrush cud one whole day during the Danger Cave excavations and though he was coursing across the heated landscape all the while, found the chewing a good mouth-conditioner, and was able to go without other nourishment and with-out exhaustion or discomfort. Of course such quids are not a self-sufficient diet. But they would, apparently, prevent starvation over short crises in food getting, and the 1000 or so found in the Wendover Caves indicate many otherwise food skimpy days.

Judging from the frequency of projectile points at four of the five levels at Danger Cave, hunting was a cus-tomary task. One weakly stemmed point only was found in the lowest, 11-000-year-old stratum, but this is enough to show that fluted points were not the only kind being used at that period. Sharpened shafts without stone points may have been considered sufficient at the time; they certainly were in use later. Early shafts may have been javelins, the atlatl or spear thrower not being certainly present until about 9000 years ago, with the bow and arrow coming much later. To this game-taking equipment must be added snares and traps. One wooden snare was found in the highest level; but, considering the ingeniousness of the Danger Cavers, these must have been ancient devices.

There is nothing unusual about this hunting equipment at Danger Cave, nor anything distinctive about the stone-work, except that nothing like any of the herd-hunter point styles—the Clovis and Folsom, for example—were made. What is remarkable, in addition to the milling of small grain, are the textiles and cordage. The twined basketry found in level II (C14 date about 9400 years ago) is, according to Jennings, "among the oldest dated basketry or textile known to archaeology." And the other specimens approximately as old are from the same general region. Sandals from Fort Rock Cave in Oregon (C14 date 10,000 years ago) and twined materials from Leonard Rock Shelter and Fishbone Cave, Nevada, are equally early. Thus, Jennings says simple basketry and other weaving techniques "were widely practiced in western North America before textile work was known in the Eurasiatic Neolithic."

Cordage of vegetable fiber, showing the overhand knot and the girth hitch, was found in the bottom level

of Danger Cave. This is sufficient to establish its manufacture and use earlier than there is record of elsewhere.
Aside from the usual binding uses, cordage was used both
for tump lines and to make netting for string bags. This
kind of material is profuse enough throughout the 8000
years of occupation though it is rare in the lowest level,
which is the one we are concerned with in this chapter.
Its presence there at all is what counts.

What we have at Danger Cave, it seems, at about
11,000 years ago, is nothing that we could fit neatly into
Old World classifications. It is "Mesolithic" in general
living pattern, but its milling of small grain brings it to
the very edge of the Neolithic. It shares with the Old
World Mesolithic an almost total disregard for art and
decoration. Yet its flint-smithing is not the blade techn-
nique of either the late Paleolithic or the Mesolithic; it is
the old-fashioned percussion method. The tool inventory
is nondescript: points, scrapers, knives, drills, possible
gravers, abrading or rubbing stones, hammerstones and
choppers, the latter a survivor from a much earlier day.
There were no axes or burins or woodworking tools (the
area was practically treeless), though there were awls,
needles and other pieces of horn, antler and bone. Crude
gaming pieces were found, but nothing that would suggest a rich ceremonial life. Fiber sandals were dug out,
too, but nothing to suggest what else, if anything else,
was worn. There was cloth of rabbit and other animal
hair mixed with vegetable fiber, probably for blankets,
but no care for color. And there were beds of grass or

bark, but no man-made roof to raise over them.

The early Paleolithic all over the world was mainly a scavenging kind of existence. The Desert Culture people of Danger Cave raised scrounging to an art, but because they never took the next step they remained essentially Paleolithic. In a sense this is the direction of development that finally brought man to civilization because it taught him to use every resource of the world around him and to look for more. As we have seen, hunting was not the road to civilization. Yet it was a necessary road for a while because it established and spread man as a species, during the late Paleolithic period. It gave him a chance to find out what was in him. When he then had to return to hunting-gathering he made the most of it. That is, some men did. But the scanty resources of the Great Basin would not support a large enough population to give birth to a civilization which seems to require, at a minimum, a sizeable population permanently settled and in control of a dependable food supply. The Danger Cave people do not fit this definition. They are, however, the best Paleolithic people archaeology has ever unearthed.

17

America's Oldest Known Inhabitant

WHERE DID the Desert Culture people come from? The logic of their being the descendants of the much more primitive Tule Springs scavengers of Nevada has already been touched on. The problem is that the date of the Tule Springs people 30,000 or more years ago places them in southern North America at the time the Wisconsin glacier lay across Canada. Since man, coming from Asia, had to cross Canada to get to the Great Basin and other southerly climes, he could only have come, if he were here 30,000 years ago, before the Wisconsin closed off the Canadian pathways.

Some authorities do not believe man would have come to America at so early a date. At this time the Neanderthals dominated Europe and the descendants of the species called Sinanthropus or Peking Man, considered by many authorities to be Neanderthal's cousin, probably dominated eastern Asia. Nothing authentically Neanderthal has been found in any corner of America.

In consequence the Tule Springs site is often ignored or rejected as producing not sufficiently convincing evidence of human activity. It is not an archaeologist's dream site. The excavator, Mark R. Harrington, found what he believes are two campsites, one about 625 feet by 200 feet, and the other not much smaller. Within these areas he found a chopper, two scrapers, two chipped discoidal stones, and some pointed tools of

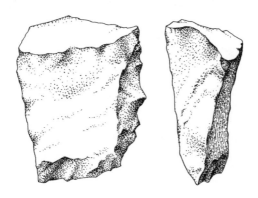

STONE CHOPPER

The chopper, simply a broad-edged hand stone, was very likely the first formalized tool of stone made by man. This example, found on the shore of the Hudson River, is perhaps 3,000 years old.

splintered bone. This can hardly be called a large inventory. It must be taken together with the bones left behind as garbage— of the camel, extinct horse, mammoth and extinct deer—and the scattered charcoal of ancient fires, to make a picture of Tule Springs. When it is considered that these two camping grounds were on the shores of a now extinct lake and that the lake rose once, before it became extinct, and covered the camps, it is easy to guess what critics will say. They will point out that the site is not undisturbed, that the dated charcoal was not from a hearth or a campfire and so does not need to be the ash of a man-made fire, that the tools need not be in association with the bones, or the tools and bones with the charcoal that produced the date, and that even if the bones had been splintered by man (to get at the marrow fat) the mammoth and horse did not become extinct until about 10,000 years ago.

These are legitimate aproaches to criticism but they are not necessarily fatal to acceptance of a Tule Springs people. Whether the charcoal actually dates them or not, they certainly did exist, did splinter the bones and must have made the artifacts, few as these are. And the very scarcity and crudeness of artifacts gives us a picture of a people primitive enough to be 30,000 years old. Therefore more and more archaeologists find Tule Springs to be a valid site of early American occupation, and a very important though unsatisfactory one.

On Tule Springs, as interpreted by its excavator and other archaeologists, rests much of the case for man's having been in America south of the Wisconsin glacier. This is construed as meaning he must have entered America before the coast-to-coast formation of the Wisconsin, about which there are two schools of thought. One school believes the period of the Wisconsin was between 30,000 and 40,000 years' duration. Another school believes it to have taken between 60,000 and 80,000 years to form, spread, retreat and vanish. But all during this period there was a way open into America from Asia around this glacier. This route lay along the Pacific Coast. That we will ever find evidence of the use of this route seems hopeless. Our Fairbridge scale has shown us that during Wisconsin times sea level was as much as 320 feet below what it is now. The seashore route from Asia is thus hidden under many fathoms of water and it seems impossible that we will ever be able to track along it, short of the invention of an archaeological submarine, to see whether or not it was used. D. M. Hopkins, the geologist, has shown that where the continents of Asia and North America are now separated at Bering Strait and the Bering Sea there was, at the high point of the Wisconsin glacier, a province of land 1000 miles wide from north to south. A great deal of archaeology must lie unattainable in its sea-buried soils.

Tule Springs is not the only or the oldest of the sites where man seems to have left his mark in America. And whereas the charcoal there was open to question, that at the Lewisville, Texas, site was not only in one hearth but in 21 hearths.

The site, on the bank of Elm Fork of the Trinity River, was actually the uncovery (rather than the discovery) of the U.S. Corps of Engineers. They were digging a gigantic borrow pit (a hole from which earth has been "borrowed" for use elsewhere) for a government dam in a terrace about 70 feet above the river. The discovery was made in the early 1950s by paleontologist Theodore E. White, who was looking for the bones of extinct animals, when the pit had reached a depth of about 20 feet. Since this leaves the site some 50 feet above the present river bed, Elm Fork has cut its bed approximately by this much since the hearths were on its banks.

The C14 dates confirm this expected age. There was plenty of datable material in both the large and small hearths. Refuse bones of large animals seem to have been associated with the larger hearths (the largest was 8 feet in diameter and 32 inches deep) while about the smaller hearths, 30 inches in diameter and 8 inches in depth, hackberry seeds and snail shells were in pronounced concentration. The smaller hearths would thus seem to represent days of slim pickings, and small hearths were in the majority. The human use of these fire pits can hardly be doubted. Therefore the date assigned them by the C14 laboratory of The Humble Oil Company raised more than one eyebrow. It was *more than* 37,000 years ago. This means that it was older than the oldest limit the laboratory was able to attain at the time. Later improved techniques—and the abundance of datable material— enabled another test to be run that is reported to have yielded a date of at least 38,000 years.

Everything was in order for such a date. Many species of animals that still inhabit the area were found—wolf, coyote, bear, deer, prairie dogs, rabbits, squirrels, mice, among others. And so were the appropriate extinct forms —horse, camel, mammoth, an extinct peccary (a piglike animal) and two species of large extinct terrapins. As a matter of fact terrapins or land turtles seem to have been on the menu with depressing regularity. The diet as a whole was that of scavenging man. There were no whole large animals, only parts, as though only a part could be salvaged from the kill of one of the large carnivores. The finds of a bison skull and a camel skull were most interesting. The skull of a kill is exactly what a carnivore would have to leave because he cannot readily get at the brain-food within. But man can.

Practically everything that walked, crawled, wiggled, flew or swam found its way into the mouth of the Lewisville Man, to judge from the bone scraps: snakes, lizards, crayfish, fish, skinks, raccoons, birds and their eggs, wolf, coyote, and snails. Lewisville Man was usually hungry enough to eat anything. The scarcity of artifacts reveals why. The chopper, that first tool type of ancient man, three flake scrapers and a hammerstone, the artifact recoveries at Lewisville, make up the inventory of man just as he crosses the threshold of tool-making and using.

What, then, was a Clovis fluted point doing beside Hearth #1? Clovis points should not be found with choppers, and they certainly should not be found beside hearths more than 37,000 years old. Clovis points have been C14 dated as late as 10,000 years ago. It has been estimated that they may be 15,000 to 18,000 years old. But as old as 38,000 years? It is unbelievable that the same type of point would have been made for more than 29,000 years.

Nevertheless, there it lay, according to all official reports, beside Hearth #1 in clay that had been heated red by a barbecue fire. Had it not been found the Lewisville site, with its 38,000-year date, would have sat much better with the authorities. Most Clovis points have been found at sites of kills, as at Naco and Lehner Ranch, and the Lewisville site is not the location of a hunting kill. They do not, of course, *have* to be found with kills, but when they *are* found at campsites, more typically Clovisian tools ought to be found with them. Generally speaking, Lewisville is not a Clovis site by anything found there except the Clovis point. Some authorities suspect that the point ought not be there and will some day be explained into another era.

Other authorities say that the point is all right and everything else will simply have to fall in line with it. Since Clovis points elsewhere have been dated at no earlier than 12,000 years ago, the whole site, hearths and all, must be only 12,000 years old. If there were any doubt about the hearths, about the adequacy of the datable material or about the geology, this position would be allowable. But it seems hasty to cast doubt on the reliability of C14 dating, built up now by over a decade's work, all for one Clovis point.

By any reasonable view, Lewisville Man of the band that had to eat hackberries, snails and terrapin so often has to be reckoned America's oldest known inhabitant, at 38,000 years of age. Some day, probably very soon, we will know the full Lewisville date. Theoretically C14 can give dates up to about 70,000 years. So far no American laboratory has been able to do better than about 40,000, but the technique is constantly improving. It would be a shock if Lewisville Man were more than 70,000 years old.

As it is, Lewisville Man is America's counterpart to the lower, or older, Paleolith men elsewhere in the world. His ancestors must have entered America before the Wisconsin no matter whether it is figured by the long count or the short. Even so, from what we know of him he is certainly a retarded type. It must have been something in the American air that enabled his descendants to become the clever Desert Culture people even though they were no more than Paleolithians themselves.

18

The Biggest Archaeological Site in the World

IN OLD WORLD ARCHAEOLOGY the stone industry
called Mousterian is usually placed in the lower or
early Paleolithic era. But if there is a middle Paleolithic,
the Mousterian is it, and there is a growing tendency
to call it that.

The Mousterian period is the time of the dominance
of the Neanderthals, quite rightly called "cave men"
though wrongly low-rated as such. It receives its name
from the site of LeMoustier in France where the skeleton

of a 15-year-old Neanderthal youth was excavated in 1906 together with Mousterian-type tools made on stone flakes. This association of tool type and Neanderthaloid skeletal material has been found to have been consistent for perhaps 100,000 years. The archaeologist Ralph Solecki excavated, between 1951 and 1960, the eastern-most appearance of Neanderthal on record, Teshik Tash in Uzbekistan. Both Mousterian tools and Neanderthal remains were discovered in context at a depth in the deposit estimated to be 70,000 years old.

At the western extremity, to choose at random, is the Spanish Cave, Cueva de la Cariguela, dug in 1955–56, where the appearance, in the bottom levels, of Mous-terian flake tools was confirmed by the discovery of three pieces of Neanderthal skull. The archaeologist C. Aram-bourg has discovered Mousterian tools in three caves in Algiers. Since the word Neanderthal comes from the Neanderthal Valley in Germany (the site is near Düssel-dorf) where the first skeletal material of this race was found, we can draw a rough outline of the territory it occupied. This was quite extensive, and the period of occupation was quite long. Neanderthals are thought to have entered and taken up residence in caves of this vast region before the last glaciation, the Würm, and may date from as early as 150,000 years ago.

The date of Neanderthal extinction, it is generally agreed, is the date of his meeting with *Homo sapiens,* man of our anatomical race (which includes all modern races of whatever color with the possible exception of

Chronology Chart

YEARS AGO	THE OLD WORLD	THE CLIMATE	THE NEW WORLD
1,820,000	Homo habilis	Wet, possibly glacial	
1,750,000	Zinjanthropus		
1,000,000		Gunz or Nebraskan Glacier	
500,000	Clactonian Man	Interglacial	
400,000	Chellean Man	Mindel or Kansan Glacier	
350,000	Pithecanthropus Erectus		
300,000	Peking Man (Sinanthropus)	Interglacial	
250,000	Swanscombe (Acheulean) Man		
200,000		Riss or Illinoisan Glacier	
100,000	Neanderthal (Mousterian) Man	Interglacial Wurm or Wisconsin Glacier	
70,000			
38,000		Warm interval	
34,000	Aurignacian (Cro-Magnon) Man	In the Wisconsin	Lewisville Man
12,000		Cool	Tule Springs Man
			Clovis Mammoth killers

Date	Event	Climate	American Culture
11,000		Warm; the Wisconsin begins to melt	The Desert Culture
9,000	Jarmo Farmers	Cool	
8,000	The Maglemosians	Cool	
5,000	The Harappans		
4,500	The Battle-Ax People	Warm	Wapanucket Villagers
4,000	First Neolithic Farmers at Jarlshof		
3,800	Megalithic Missionaries at Stonehenge		
2,800	Late Bronze Age at Jarlshof	Cool	Poverty Point people
2,600	Celts in Britain		
2,400	Iron Age at Jarlshof	Warm	
2,300			Hopewellians
2,000	Birth of Christ		
A.D. 1	Broch Tower Builders at Jarlshof	Cool	
625	Ship at Sutton Hoo		
800	Vikings at Jarlshof	Warm	
850	The King's Ship		
1300	The Sands Move in on Jarlshof		

the African Bushman)—roughly about 40,000 years ago.

These factors define the Middle Paleolithic: the Würm glacier lies across northern Europe; Neanderthal Man, who has learned to live in cold climates by sheltering in caves, by knowledge of fire making and by wearing skins, has been able to establish himself in regions shunned by warmth-loving *Homo sapiens;* he makes stone tools out of the flakes he strikes from lumps of stone which, when reduced by flaking, are called tortoise cores, from their shape. The uniformity of the Mousterian culture is remarkable over the region where Neanderthal Man lived and through the long epoch during which he lived. He was, relatively speaking, numerous, and much more Neanderthal skeletal material has been unearthed than of all other types of ancient men put together.

The full human status of this mid-Paleolithic Man, differing in many details of anatomy from Modern Man, is indisputable, however. He seems to have been the first man to practice deliberate burial, with red ochre and grave furnishings of food and tools, indicative very probably of belief in a life beyond the grave—certainly a most human trait.

Neanderthal Man having now been placed and time-scaled, we are free to dig beneath him and descend into the lower, or early, Paleolithic in that region of earth where Neanderthal's rival seems to have come from. This has to be Africa, on the evidence of the stone tools found there throughout all of prehistory, on the deduction that

Homo sapiens was a camper under the open sky until he learned cave dwelling from Neanderthal Man, and finally on the want of evidence elsewhere. And when we talk about the early Paleolithic in Africa we are talking about Olduvai Gorge.

Olduvai Gorge is the biggest archaeological site in the world. Very few places in the world have the bigness to surpass it, and so far none of them has proved to be archaeological. It is a 25-mile-long canyon in Tanganyika, East Africa, the 300-foot high walls of which are made up of the geological formations of the last million and three-quarters years. In these formations are the stone tools of the men who lived through that incredible span of time, 500 times the length of the Christian era.

It is but a part of the charm—archaeological charm, since nobody could call this rugged and mighty slash in a scorched landscape charming in appearance—that Olduvai Gorge is almost inaccessible. L. S. B. Leakey, who has been excavating there for the past three decades, reports that when he made his first expedition to Olduvai in 1931, it took two days of the hardest driving to make the last 60 miles.

He had never seen the place before, though he had been doing archaeological work in nearby Kenya for years, but he was so sure he would find traces of Paleolithic men there that he had committed most of his research funds to the expedition. He was sure despite the fact that he was told by Hans Reck, a noted German geologist who had been to Olduvai on foot, that positively no such thing could be expected.

Reck had not only been to Olduvai, he had spent a season there, digging up the fossil bones of ancient animals while studying the geology. It was he, making a second trip for fossils, with whom Leakey had joined up to make his first trip to Olduvai. The result of the difference of opinion was a friendly side-bet between the man who had been there and who said there were no signs of Paleolithic Man at Olduvai, and the man who had never been there and who said there were. Moreover, Leakey said he would find Paleolithic evidence within 24 hours of arrival. The bet was 100 pounds, at a time when the pound was worth about $5 in American money.

The party arrived about noon, had lunch, set up camp, and before nightfall, within 100 yards of camp, Leakey had picked up half a dozen signs of the Paleolithic, including hand-axes. He does admit he was lucky.

The artifact-bearing walls of the gorge consist of five beds or strata representing five major climatic periods, all resting on a bed consisting of a very, very ancient lava flow. As things are now figured, these five beds cover approximately the whole Ice Age period of the four great glaciers (in the Old World called the Günz, Mindel, Riss and Würm, and in America called the Nebraskan, Kansan, Illinoisian and the Wisconsin). But in Africa the Ice Age periods produced no glaciation. It is thought more likely that they were periods of heavy rainfall, called pluvials.

Remains of more than 100 species of animals are found throughout these beds. Most of these animals are still in existence, but some are not. Perhaps we would recognize the elephants of that day, since this is Africa and we would be expecting elephants, and perhaps we wouldn't. The modern elephant wasn't there; but an ancestor, *Paleoloxodon antiquus,* was. So was another one, dinotherium, with short tusks curving down out of his lower jaw, instead of curving up, or sticking straight out of his upper jaw, as in more conventional types.

There are no wild horses in Africa today (not counting the zebra), but there were in the old days—a three-toed model called hipparion. Hippopatomi were plentiful and about as one would expect them, except for the giant Hippopatomas Gorgops, whose periscope eyes were on top of and higher than his head. There was a giant size in everything. Among eight species of pigs was one as big as a rhinoceros. Among many kinds of bovids—that is, the ox family—was a sheep as big as a buffalo, with seven-foot horns. Simopithecus was a baboon more than twice as big as the modern baboon. Besides little hipparion and a zebra and two other horse types there was one considerably bigger than any modern wild horse. Sivatherium was a giraffe, and a very strange one, with shorter legs, a shorter neck and a much heavier body than our circus and zoo type, and immense antler-like things sprouting from his head.

The most astonishing beast of all, however, was a chalicothere (a long extinct line) called metaschizotherium. (Incidentally, you will have little trouble with some of these names if you remember that "there" or "therium" merely means beast and is applied to archaic, now-extinct forms only.) His teeth were those of an ungulate; that is, a grazing or browsing animal, like a cow or deer, which has hooves. But instead of hooves he had a five-toed, clawed foot, like a carnivorous, preying animal, such as a tiger. The herbiage-chewing teeth and the claws, in biological experience, are plain contradictions of each other. In consequence the chalicothere claws have been interpreted as adapted to digging up roots. The chalicotheres were very odd-appearing animals which look as though they had been put together by an amateur anatomist. The head was horselike, but rather smaller, proportionately, since the body was much heavier than a modern horse's, while the legs were like those of a giraffe, long in front and short in the rear.

Yet there was nothing unique about this African chalicothere. Relatives are found widely throughout the world, including an American cousin called moropus, and the type existed through millions of years. While most archaic animals still exist in some modern form, extinct forms like the chalicotheres raise an interesting question. Had they continued to exist in some form, what use would they have been put to by man? Would chalicothere have made a good pet, or a draft animal, or a dairy or meat animal? Or would he have been only a nuisance, to be exterminated?

As Leakey and his co-workers, including his wife, Mary, toiled away through the decades, dissecting the

Olduvai site, they found remains of those and other animals in the five geological beds.

There is no permanent stream in Olduvai Gorge now, but the infrequent storm rains can quickly pour into the gorge a river of torrential force. The situation is familiar to those who know the arroyos of our arid West, dry all year except for a few hours when floods that can drown beasts and men gush through them.

It is certain that tool-making manlike beings lived in Africa during the formation and disappearance of the four great glaciers of the Ice Age. By reason of their animal-like living habits, these Africans must have gone north with the retreat of the glaciers, and thus become Europeans. When glaciers formed and pushed climatic zones southward, man must have returned to Africa with the southward verging of his food without any suspicion that he was shifting from one continent to another.

The earliest tools found at Olduvai are still not the earliest stone tools made by man. To look at them, though, is to think there could hardly be anything simpler. They are pebble "choppers," river pebbles shaped to a single cutting edge.

The next step in the development of the chopper is the logical one, chipping a cutting edge from both sides of the pebble. These are called Oldowan choppers and are the earliest certain stone tools of human manufacture. With these we are on the way to hand-axes, the most widely distributed tool over the longest period of time in the career of man. East of India the chopper remained the principal tool of Paleolithic Man and we have mentioned it as occurring in America. Everywhere else hand-axes succeeded the chopper as Paleolithic Man's standard tool.

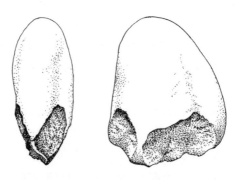

PEBBLE CHOPPER

This pebble chopper can be and probably was made in 30 seconds or less, by striking off four flakes, two on each side but not opposite each other, so that the cutting edge is scalloped. Pebble choppers appear at the very bottom of stone industry at Olduvai.

The hand-ax proper appears at the beginning of the formation of Bed II at Olduvai. It is by now an approximately pear-shaped or beet-shaped tool. The pebble selected for working was chipped down from all sides to a two-sided tool, the sides being approximately flat. Often a little of the smooth pebble "rind" or outside was left at the top or butt to protect the hand of the user. The hand-ax was never hafted.

Early hand-axes were rough and clumsy-looking, their edges, where the two sides meet, not being particularly sharp or straight. The natural question that arises is,

228

what good were they? Leakey, a genuine expert in stone tools, demonstrated not long ago how good they were in the hands of an expert. With a flint chopper made by himself out of a casual pebble in 30 seconds, he skinned and cut up the carcass of a full-grown ram in less than 20 minutes.

The next step in stone technology is the use of the "soft hammer" of bone, antler or hardened wood instead of stone. The soft hammer gave the artisan better control of flaking and the hand-ax became thinner, true-edged, better outlined and, in many specimens, beautiful. Some of them even seem to have been made for no other reason since they were too fragile and even too large for use.

This hand-ax is well established by the time Bed IV was laid down at Olduvai and the cleaver—a broad-bitted tool with hand-grasp at right angles to the blade, like a hoe—is added to the tool inventory. So rapid (comparatively speaking) does technical progress become that at the top of Bed IV Olduvai men have reached a higher level and we are in the late Paleolithic age.

It should be noted here, perhaps, that hand-axes are not absent from America, though nobody knows where they belong in time or what they mean. What we need in America is at least a minor Olduvai with all our culture periods stacked neatly on top of one another. Such a site would do much to settle the question of how long has been man's residency of the Western Hemisphere.

Any thought about the hand-ax will lead eventually to the conclusion that it is not an habitual hunting weapon because, being held in the hand, it does not get the hunter near enough to his game, nor has it any killing advantage. There is but one way in which it could have been used as a hunting weapon. The hunter would have to lie in ambush, preferably in a tree or on a high rock, and drop physically on his game—the way the fabulous Tarzan attacked lions—using the hand-ax to break the neck of the quarry or deal some other mortal blow. Yet there is nothing in archaeology to show that man did his hunting in this way.

Instead, from the time of Chellean Man, the first hand-ax maker, the Olduvai hunters used the cleverest device ever thought up for more or less painless hunting —the bolas. We have already encountered the bolas at Poverty Point and we know that the device is used even today by Argentinian cowboys and Eskimos. We hardly expect to find it so long ago in man's past. But Leakey finds stone balls of many sizes suitable for bolas and explicable in no other way. They have even been found nested together in threes.

A proper cast of the bolas at the legs of a running animal can bring it down and stun it long enough for the hunter to rush in with hand-ax or pointed wooden spear to make his kill. A swirling bola stone, wrapped by its cords around the legs, can easily break a leg bone; and a broken-legged animal in the wild is as good as dead.

From the size of the stones identified as bolas at Olduvai, Leakey surmises that Chellean Man was a powerful fellow. The big bolas would indicate he hunted big, stout-legged game. And Leakey's long years of excavation have shown that he did hunt the giant pig, the antlered giraffe and the giant sheep. The bones of one Chellean feast proved to be that of so huge a dinotherium —the elephant with the down-curving tusks in his under-jaw—that a new scientific name has to be found for him. One species of dinotherium having been called *maximus,* the greatest, and a bigger one found later having been called *gigantissimus,* the most gigantic, the Olduvai specimen which is distinctly bigger still has no word left for him in the Latin dictionary. Leakey is trying *mirabilis* —that is, awesome or astounding.

Through the length of archaeological time at Olduvai, then, man was a tool-maker who slowly but continuously improved his tools and by this process made himself more and more modern—in looks, anatomy, intellect, imagination, speech and social organization.

So what about him? Among the bones of more than 100 species of animals dug out of Olduvai, was there not one of Paleolithic Man? In 1913 Reck dug a well-preserved skeleton out of Bed II, which would have made the man who once dragged those bones about as of Chellean age. But exhaustive investigation showed him to have been not even late Paleolithic. After that, the only human things that Leakey had to show for more than 20 seasons of excavation were a couple of milk teeth.

Until 1959.

Until July 17, 1959, to be exact.

19

The End Is the Beginning

LEAKEY HIMSELF WAS SICK on July 17, 1959, and his wife, having ordered him to bed, fared forth herself to do the family fossil hunting, since the digging season was nearing its close. It seemed she had barely got to her diggings when she was back with news that jolted Leakey upright from his cot.

"I've got him!" Mrs. Leakey said. And Leakey, who had been searching for "him" for 28 years, knew exactly what she meant—a human skull in Bed I.

Then Mrs. Leakey showed her husband where it lay, embedded in the earth, its teeth gleaming in the sunlight. It was within yards of the place where Leakey, on that first day at Olduvai in 1931, had found the hand-axes that had won the bet from Reck.

For the next 19 days the Leakeys worked with dental picks, camel's-hair brushes and sieves, and by the end of that time they had recovered 400 pieces of a skull complete except for the lower jaw. Inside this skull had been the brain guiding the hands that had made the Bed I choppers.

The most noticeable fact about the skull, as the Leakeys toiled over it, was the size of the teeth. The molars and pre-molars were flat-crowned and extraordinarily large, the largest molars ever found in a human skull. These were teeth made for the mastication of a coarse vegetable diet. But the front teeth, the biting teeth, were relatively small, almost of human size.

By its teeth alone this Bed I skull was a far cry from the animal, in that it no longer had the wild animal's protective equipment. This was the dentition of an eater who was both herbivorous and carnivorous, the tooth development of a hunter-collector who depended on no special diet but who would eat anything and everything that would nourish his body. Here, in the biological sculpture of anatomy, was the kind of human-like creature who had set the pattern of livelihood for all mankind. Though man, we know, made his advances through the Paleolithic period as a hunter, when game grew scarce he had his taste for and knowledge of vegetal foods to fall back on, and so invented agriculture. But he never lost his taste for meat, either, and to satisfy it he invented animal husbandry.

233

Reconstructed, the Bed I skull of this pebble-chopper-maker presents the anthropologist with a hominid (human-like) cranium and countenance entirely new, yet by no means unexpected. It is not modern man; the forehead is very low and the skull is crowned with a sagittal crest, a front-to-back bony ridge which supports the jaw muscles. It certainly is not of the brow-ridged Pithecan-thropus line, which is noted for prognathism or jutting forward of the mouth-nose or muzzle region of the face. Because this hominid walked as erectly as modern man, had nearly even front teeth, and had his face nearly in a vertical plane, he could not be placed near the apes. To Leakey the conclusion is inescapable. The Bed I skull belonged to a form beyond the Australopithicine group and at least halfway in cranial characteristics to *Homo sapiens*.

So Leakey called his Bed I hominid Zinjanthropus—East Africa Man—and his position as the earliest human being seemed secure.

But in 1961 something entirely new and different turned up, *below* Zinjanthropus in Bed I, and therefore earlier, yet in many respects more advanced along the line of human development. This find consisted, when all the evidence was in, of the jaw, with teeth, some cranial parts, enough finger bones to reconstruct a hand, and some foot bones. The bones were those of a youth under sixteen years of age who had been killed by a head blow.

Between 1961 and 1964 several further finds of this

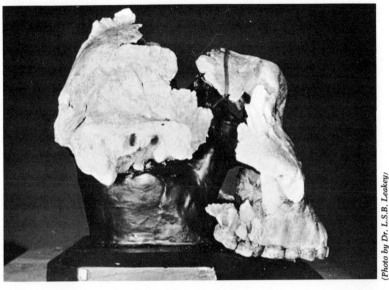

(Photo by Dr. L.S.B. Leakey)

ZINJANTHROPUS

This is the skull of Zinjanthropus as mounted by Dr. Leakey after recovery of both the occiput and frontal bones including the upper jaw but lacking the lower jaw, which was not found. The mounting shows very well the unusual flat-headedness and narrow forehead of Zinjanthropus.

pre-Zinjanthropus race were made. Enough skeletal material was added to the original collection to make it possible to define the race. It is, indeed, more directly in the line of our ancestry, with hands and feet much nearer our own in anatomic structure. Whereas the big molars and pre-molars of Zinjanthropus were better suited for the mastication of vegetal food, the pre-Zinjanthropus people had smaller teeth adapted to biting and chewing both vegetal and animal substances. So

235

certain did Leakey become about the "humanity" of the pre-Zinjanthropus race that he named it *Homo habilis*, which means able or capable or even handy man. As Leakey now figures it Zinjanthropus and *Homo habilis* must have lived side by side for hundreds of thousands of years. And then Zinjanthropus died out.

From his 30 years of knowledge of Olduvai geology Leakey estimated the age of Zinjanthropus at 600,000 years, an age that pushed mankind back 100,000 years beyond the usual run of such estimates. But he did not depend on geological estimate alone. Rock of an age equivalent with the skull was sent to the Department of Geology, University of California, for age tests by the relatively new potassium-argon method.

In principle this method is much like the C14 method, being dependent on the decay of radioactive materials. As we already know, C14 can be used, theoretically, for the dating of materials no older than about 70,000 years. Potassium 40, however, has the half-life capacity to fix dates in millions of years.

In May, 1961, the potassium 40 tests were complete and Garniss H. Curtis who, with his partner Jack F. Evernden had supervised them, wrote Leakey that Zinjanthropus was at least 1,750,000 years old. (*Homo habilis*, found below Zinjanthropus, must then be about 1,820,000 years old.)

The meaning of this dating of Zinjanthropus to archaeology and geology is such that many authorities, perhaps most, hesitate to accept it. The validity of the dating does not, however, depend on how many authorities accept it. If there is nothing wrong with the potassium 40 method of dating—its half-life may be inaccurately known, for instance; and there was nothing wrong with the laboratory procedure during the tests (two were run and the 1,750,000 years is the average of the two); and there was no mistake in collecting the rock for the tests; then no amount of authoritative skepticism can subtract a year from Zinjanthropus's age.

On the other hand an enormous amount of investigation and study has gone into the conclusion that Leakey reached in the first place—that Zinjanthropus is about 600,000 years old. This date is probably acceptable to most authorities. Before this well-reasoned conclusion is upset, making it necessary to re-write all geological and archaeological texts, the potassium 40 result must be checked again and again, until there is only a minor possibility that it is wrong.

Aside from this question of how old Zinjanthropus and *Homo habilis* are, and that other question of the definition of humanity, the Bed I skull of the *Homo habilis* youth who probably died in mankind's earliest murder mystery, is the oldest skull of a human tool-maker ever uncovered. Its anatomical characteristics are as primitive as the culture it was found with. On these known facts its importance rests, and that importance is not likely to be destroyed.

After the discovery of Zinjanthropus, The National Geographic Society (of the United States) made generous provision for the Leakeys to continue excavation at Olduvai. Whereas formerly they had been able to dig only about seven weeks a year, with the National Geographic Society's grant the Leakeys undertook to work the whole year through. In one period of 13 months they were able to do more than twice as much excavating and exploring as in the previous 30 years.

The results were worth it. Since 1961 Leakey has been able to announce more discoveries of Zinjanthropus and *Homo habilis*, with tools and other cultural evidence to prove how handy *Homo habilis* was. These finds, taken together with the skeletal discovery of Chellean Man, prove to the satisfaction of most authorities that East Africa was the birthplace of our human stock. More finds can be expected to come from the treasure house of Olduvai Gorge, of which Leakey is the keeper.

The discovery of Chellean Man is important because he was the maker of the first hand-axes, man's first really formal tool. A Chellean skull was found, with hand-axes, in Bed II above Zinjanthropus. It is the first such skeletal evidence of a Chellean ever encountered. In association with the Chellean, on one of his living floors, were found lumps of red ochre—that bright thread of pigment that runs through man's story from 400,000 years ago, through Neanderthal times and into the burials of the Hopewellians. Man has been the maker, the color dauber, the artist, from the beginning.

What is ironic about this discovery of the skull of Chellean Man is that his tools were the first evidences of Paleolithic Man ever discovered. They can be said to have initiated the subject of Paleolithic archaeology. The name Chellean derives from Chelles, France, where, in 1846, Boucher de Perthes, the founding father of the notion that man had lived during the glacial epochs, first recognized that certain chipped stones found in river gravels were tools intentionally shaped by man and gave them the name *coup de poing* (from the French, blow of the fist), or hand-ax. During the more than a century since then the kind of hand-ax or *coup de poing* fashioned by Chellean Man has been found from England to India. But no skeletal part of the maker had ever come to light.

Leakey describes his Chellean Man of Bed II as having had the most massive brow of any known early man, having reconstructed his cranium from a total of thirteen pieces of skull recovered. In this application the word "man" is used with the utmost confidence. Some authorities may dispute that either Zinjanthropus or *Homo habilis* may accurately be called man. In the case of Chellean Man there is no argument. The fact that his hand-axes were fully realized, if rudimentary, tools made by the same repetitive methods that had to be passed on by a teaching generation to a learning generation for over a hundred thousand years settles the question. An anthropoid becomes a man when he becomes a tool-maker.

The hand-ax was not the only tool made by Chellean Man. To have been a hunter, which Chellean Man was, judging from the amount of bones of large animals found on his living floors, he needed a hunting weapon. The hand-ax, useful as it was in cutting up game and in many other food-getting activities, was no such weapon. Leakey is sure that the hunting weapon of Chellean Man was the bolas, that arrangement of three stones tied together by thongs and thrown at the legs of game to bring it down or disable it so that it could be approached and killed. Many round pebbles have been found on the living floors of Chellean Man that would have been suitable for bolas, and Leakey has even found them nested together in threes. Some of them are so large that Leakey is sure Chellean Man must have been large and powerful. The Bed II skull bears this out.

With his bolas and his powerful build Chellean Man was a full-fledged hunter. "Countless remains of such huge animals as the giant pig, the giant antlered giraffe, the giant sheep and several other immense creatures" were found on the Chellean living floors, Leakey reports. It was Chellean Man who had eaten the dinotherium *mirabilis* mentioned earlier, though it is not suggested that he ever deliberately tackled such a monster.

There can be no doubt, then, about Chellean Man's prowess as a hunter, as a flintsmith and, in view of the red ochre, that mysterious tendency which led him in the direction somehow of religion and art. But there is going to be a great deal of hesitation about where he is to be placed in the line of human physical development. The tools of Olduvai show a steady and clear-cut evolution from chopper to hand-ax and beyond. Of the skeletal material this is hardly true. Pre-Zinjanthropus differentiates from Zinjanthropus and the 13 fragments of the skull of Chellean Man, when put together, show a completely variant type of hominid altogether. Whereas the Australopithicines and Zinjanthropus have relatively smooth foreheads the Chellean skull has "the most massive brow of any early man known."

What does all this mean? That the human line began in a form that was smooth-browed, became massively browed and then became smooth-browed again?

Or were pre-Zinjanthropus and Zinjanthropus supplanted by heavy-browed Chellean Man, as heavy-browed Neanderthal Man was much later supplanted by smooth-browed Cro-Magnons?

Or did three different lines of hominids camp on the shores of ancient Lake Olduvai at the same time, or at different times, and if they did which one is the ancestor of modern man, *Homo sapiens?* For were not all three tool-makers, and thus human and hence meriting our concern as archaeologists for their extinction or survival?

Does not the heavy brow ridge of Chellean Man relate him to Rhodesian Man, from Rhodesia, South Africa, only a little south of Tanganyika, who also had a heavy brow ridge? And may not these brow-ridged men be related to brow-ridged Neanderthal Man?

With these questions—a dozen more will probably suggest themselves to the reader—this archaeological journey backward through time must end. Because it is with questions, not answers, that a book on archaeology, indeed on any science, ought to end. This was the point made in the first chapter, that we cannot acquire knowledge without subjecting ourselves to the need for more. The prehistory of man is not a subject complete, to all intents and purposes, and circumscribed by a perfect circle of certainty. The exhilarating finds at Olduvai have raised more questions than they have answered and this is what gives archaeology its suspense. It is like a serial story, with the next chapter, no matter how full of action, always leading to the one after it.

All through this book we have encountered uncertainty —about Stonehenge, about the ship at Sutton Hoo, about the people of Poverty Point, about Lewisville Man, about Chellean Man. There really is no end to archaeology. We will meet Stonehenge again, and Lewisville Man and the hand-ax people of Olduvai, and other people whom we don't now know even exist. This is archaeology's happy ending—that there is more, much more to come.

INDEX

Index

Index

Index